The Postindustrial Promise

The Postindustrial Promise

Vital Religious Community in the 21st Century

Anthony E. Healy

THE
ALBAN
INSTITUTE

Herndon, Virginia
www.alban.org

The Alban Institute
2121 Cooperative Way, Suite 100
Herndon, VA 20171

Cover design by Adele Robey, Phoenix Graphics.

Library of Congress Cataloging-in-Publication Data

Healy, Anthony E.
 The postindustrial promise : vital religious community in the 21st century / Anthony E. Healy.
    p. cm.
 Includes bibliographical references.
 ISBN 1-56699-287-7
 1. Christian sociology—United States. 2. Social change—Religious aspects—Christianity. I. Title.

 BR517.H43 2005
 306.6'773083—dc22

                         2005001746

09 08 07 06 05   VG   1 2 3 4 5

Mimi

pax

One of the unintended consequences of modern capitalism is that it has strengthened the value of place, aroused a longing for community. All the emotional conditions we have in the workplace animate that desire: the uncertainties of flexibility; the absence of deeply rooted trust and commitment; the superficiality of teamwork; most of all, the specter of failing to make something of oneself in the world, to "get a life" through one's work. All these conditions impel people to look for some other scene of attachment and depth.

—Richard Sennett, *The Corrosion of Character*

Contents

Preface

Capturing the church's groundbreaking, the photograph on the wall had been pieced together from three successive exposures to form an elongated image. It was a happy picture. Neatly dressed children, from beaming toddlers to more somber teenagers, were lined up in an immense rank. Behind them stood smiling adults, dressed in business suits and day dresses, clutching new shovels and obviously pleased. Further emphasizing the mightiness of the children's long rank, the row of adults barely protruded out of the center image.

Four decades after the groundbreaking, a group of older members sat in the church kitchen around a worn linoleum table. They had come to hear a report about their church and its community. None of these church members lived in that community. None of them were the children in the picture that had required the two extra exposures. The report said the community around the church had changed. The community was attracting immigrants and had become ethnic. A Hispanic group was already renting their church on Sunday afternoons. The original church had shrunk to a handful of older, white adults. They could barely care for the church building. That evening, around that table and below that framed picture on the wall behind them, a long process began that led to the church's closure and the handing over of its property to the Hispanic church. Begun with so much young promise, the church had died.

This is a real story. But this story is old hat. It has appeared thousands of times in recent decades, told in many different versions and in many different places. The story has a sad ending, that is, if the fact is conveniently ignored that a Hispanic congregation rose from the ashes of this church. I tell this story not because it reflects the state of religion and congregations in America today but because it reflects the story that is being constantly told about religion and congregations in this country. Tales of demise and decline have come to characterize the state of religion and congregations. In these stories, the scapegoat for the

problems of religious bodies has become the congregations themselves.
But the story I told is not about a congregation that messed up. Mistakes
were made; opportunities were lost. After all, the congregation was made
up of humans. But the story of this church would not be essentially rewritten if at some point they had done this instead of that. Forces were
at work over which this church had no control, much less knowledge of.
The changes in religious life in the United States and among congregations are being misunderstood within the religious community, as well
as by some religious scholars. The real story of our age is not demise
and decline. The real story is about how congregations are valuable places
to people in a disordered society, places where people have rerooted
religiously and culturally in the changed social landscape of the
postindustrial transformation. Here begins that story.

We live in a time of great change. Change has touched many parts of our
lives: our families, our jobs, our neighborhoods, and our religious communities. Change has touched us from many directions: socially, economically, politically, demographically, educationally, environmentally,
technologically, and physiologically. Change has also touched many parts
of the world, from the most economically advanced global cities to the
most remote rural hamlets.

We are in a time of great religious change, too. The world's major
faiths are reconstituting their beliefs, reshaping their organizational
forms, and refortifying themselves with fresh adherents. Virtually every day, news accounts remind us that religion is still a powerful moti-
vation both to inciting violence and to easing suffering. With much less
sensation than what is often found in those news accounts, change has
also touched many local religious communities. Theological tenets, gov-
erning structure and the loyalties of congregants are being contested in
at least some fashion in most churches, parishes, synagogues, temples,
and masjids.

What happened in the last decades of the twentieth century that has
brought us to this strange new world in the early years of the twenty-
first century? To understand the changes that have occurred, I have
turned to social science. But this book does more than recite the prevailing theories current in the social sciences, especially those tagged as
postmodern. Instead, this book challenges those theories. It pictures what
has occurred in recent decades as a postindustrial transformation. This
transformation from an economy in which manufacturing was a leading employer to an economy in which many types of corporate and consumer services are the largest employer has actually had important and

often unnoticed ramifications on society that go far beyond where and how we earn our living. This transformation has changed what we value and how we live, as well as how we work. It has also changed congregations and religious life, but not necessarily in the fashion that many people have claimed.

When postmodern theorists talk about the changes in our world, they describe a society in which individualism turns extreme, social groups collapse, and tradition is scrapped, among other things. These presumed aspects of postmodern life suggest tragic outcomes for congregations and established religion. But the actual situations that sociologists of religion have encountered in a recent flurry of research among congregations and in religion suggests that this story line, as it pertains to congregations and religion, needs to be revised.

Based on the findings of these sociologists and other scholars, this book's primary theme is that people, instead of following the script postmodern theorists have prescribed, are again putting down roots religiously and socially following an epic economic change that has dislocated their lives. In putting down those roots, people are drawing on the knowledge that has been passed down to them about how life is to be lived and religion is to be practiced. Instead of traveling their own individual path religiously, most people are forming into a number of religious subcultures with distinctive values, norms, beliefs, and practices. In these subcultures, the past is often invoked in some way as a source of group solidarity.

Different from the postmodern script, this postindustrial explanation leads us to fresh insights into the change that has occurred among religious bodies, their congregants, and their immediate geographic locales. Most important, in the postindustrial explanations, congregations are the places in society in which people bring together their stories of how religion is to be practiced and society ought to be run. These stories are brought back to life and put into use within congregations. Thus, congregations are the actual places of rerooting, or of reembodying, religious and cultural narratives.

This book's secondary theme is that congregations, as a result of their role in postindustrial society, are important and vital places for people. Yet, a common wisdom that is usually negative doggedly persists within religious circles about the value of religion in society and the vitalness of congregations. This common wisdom is based on outdated theory and postmodern misinterpretations and is perpetuated by an inherent inability within religious circles to see congregations as they actually *are*.

The postindustrial explanation presents a different view of religion and congregations. That view should suggest to religious leaders new ways for religious bodies to be responsive and viable places of ministry, mission, and program.

This book is meant for religious leaders—pastors, lay leaders, teachers, scholars, and seminarians. The goal is to provide a solid grounding in the basic aspects of the postindustrial transformation and their consequences on society and religion so that religious leaders act responsively. One purpose of this book is to introduce the scholars whose recent work has helped redirect how social science views the present-day world and, in particular, to reshape sociological understandings of religion and religious communities. This book recounts changes that have occurred in the sociology of religion in recent years. These changes undercut many of the assumptions of early social science, assumptions on which religious leaders still continue to operate. I explain how the postindustrial transformation has changed society foundationally. I also examine the basics of new and emerging sociological theories that promise to displace postmodern concepts.

This book is organized into six chapters. Chapter 1 reaches into the history of sociology and explores the development of postmodern theory that currently dominates our thinking about society and communities of faith. In looking at the array of congregational self-help resources on the market, this chapter also suggests that these resources need to move on from an insistent fixation on outdated theory, if not inaccurate data. Chapter 2 focuses on the foundational changes of the postindustrial transformation and their ramifications on society and religion. This chapter looks at how the postindustrial transformation has changed social class, the workplace, and residential geography, as well as personal mobility, young adulthood, and human longevity. The chapter then explores how these changes have affected religion and its place in society.

After this broad introduction, chapter 3 turns to new explanations of the role of religion and religious bodies in society. The chapter illustrates how the postindustrial transformation has reshaped local faith communities. Religious communities have become ever more diversified in their religious backgrounds, internal demographics, organizational styles, and congregational forms. Chapter 4 explores in more depth the religious subcultures that enfold congregations and the demographic uniformity that shapes congregations. Chapter 5 offers a fresh perspective on congregational form and style. That chapter will look at sociological models of congregations and how style is a deeper issue than simply how worship is done. Chapter 6 pulls these ideas together and looks at the four challenges that confront congregations and religious leaders this century. It calls on religious leaders to reexamine their present assumptions about religion and congregations and set out in new directions.

This book contains a number of portraits of congregations. Some of these portraits are drawn from the recent work of several sociologists of religion, whose work provides the solid basis for the claim that congregations are vital and important places for people. Several other portraits come from field work done in conjunction with The Church in Postindustrial America project, which the Louisville Institute generously funded for two years, permitting me to travel to diverse congregations around the country to interview their leaders and, in some cases, to attend their services. The grant also gave me the time apart from regular work to do extensive reading and thinking. For that, I am deeply grateful to the Louisville Institute. I am also deeply grateful to the pastors, staff, congregational leaders, and others who sat down and shared valuable time with me. Some of these people and their churches appear in this book. Others do not. But the latter have not been forgotten, and their time and information were valuable to me. I pray that the material in this book will in return be helpful to their ministry and that of their congregations.

I also want to thank a number of academic colleagues who suggested particular congregations, Lowell W. Livezey of the Religion in Urban America Project in Chicago, Jon Miller of the University of Southern California, and Heidi Rolland Unruh, then of the Eastern Baptist Theological Seminary. Other congregations were suggested and more visits were planned in New York and Washington; however, 9/11 and the Iraq War impeded those planned visits. I wish to thank two friends and colleagues, Helen Berger and Elfriede Wedam, who early on read parts of this book and calmed my apprehensions about this work. Dean Hoge at the Catholic University of America and R. Stephen Warner of the University of Illinois at Chicago also provided comments. Detlef Pollack, the Max Weber Chair for German and European Studies at New York University, helpfully explained the stickier points of Niklas Luhmann's theory as it pertained to religion. And certainly, I wish to thank Carl Dudley, recently retired director of the Hartford Institute for Religion Research, for reading the final draft manuscript and for his many useful observations. I am also appreciative of the Alban Institute, and its editor, Beth Gaede, for her patience.

Not least is my deep affection for Emily, my spouse, who put up with the travel and the time away that made this work possible, and whose support in essential ways was unflagging.

As I said earlier in this introduction, this book is anchored in a foundational, scientific explanation of an important global event that has suddenly changed the way we live. This book is not a theological explanation of that event, nor is it a theological prescription of how religious communities should respond to that event. The work that I do is based on empirical studies in the social sciences and is underlined by the hard realities that confront congregations. Immersed in the social scientific world through dedicated reading, helpful academic colleagues, and steady participation in conferences, I fused together many newer ideas arising in social science that deal with religion, cities, work, and ethnicity. Most important, this book draws on 14 interesting years spent working with many different congregations in many different places and helping them to understand the people who live in the places around their buildings. This book reflects, too, the deep concern of those religious communities about the importance of their congregational life and their religious role among people in the present-day world.

Whatever else, this is decidedly an optimistic book. It contains no dire predictions. It does not fire off the tales of demise and decline of American religious life with which the preface began, and with which we are regularly bombarded. I have cast my lot with those who find that God is working in new ways and who see the emergence of a promising new social, economic, and political order despite how incredibly difficult the birth of that order has been to date. To repeat the apt words of sociologist Penny Edgell in her own book that affirms the vital role that congregations play still, this book, too, is a "cheery voice raised against the ongoing lament."[1]

Chapter 1

Getting Religion Right

Ever since sociology emerged as a social science in the nineteenth century, religion has been a key part of sociological theories about society and human relationships. Those ideas have colored scholarly notions about religion until recent decades. But as I show in this chapter, long-standing sociological theories about secularization and religious pluralism have turned out not to be entirely sound. Confronted with new social and economic developments, as well as the failure of these earlier sociological theories, sociologists in the latter part of the twentieth century rewrote theories about the role of religion in what social scientists now call a postmodern society.

But problems have surfaced, too, with this postmodern theory. Scholarly doubts are growing about whether the religious changes that postmodern theory describes are actually occurring across the bulk of society. Yet, despite its flaws, postmodern theory, as well as the old theories, still informs the views of many pastors and religious leaders about religion and congregational life. The incessant tales of religious demise and decline, for example, and a mistaken notion of congregations as out-of-it organizations in need of drastic overhaul, for another example, are the result. In fact, much of the congregational self-help material used by thousands of congregations and millions of religious leaders continues to hew to this misplaced conventional wisdom about religion and congregations.

In this chapter, I outline the major changes that have occurred in the sociology of religion, many of which have escaped the attention of the religious community. The chapter also lays the basis for understanding the state of religion and religious congregations from a different perspective. In this different perspective, religion plays an important role in society, and as several recent sociological studies of congregations have shown, congregations are important and vital places for people.

1

The Dawning of the Modern World

As pictured by the pioneers of sociology, among them Max Weber of Germany and Emile Durkheim of France, the modern world was the consequence of industrialism. Industrialism was the economic force that shaped the nineteenth century, especially in Europe, the time and place in which these two scholars worked. Industrialism brought on a new way of life for Europeans and Americans. Individually crafted goods were replaced by standardized manufactured goods. Many of these manufactured goods were produced in factories with hundreds of laborers. These factories spawned huge, new industrial cities. As these cities drew people in from the countryside, the old ways of rural life on which European society had rested for many centuries were replaced by the new ways of urban life.

Besides a shift to work in the factory and life in the city, industrialism also brought about a reliance on science and technology. Industrialism arrived in the aftermath of the Enlightenment, a philosophical revolution that sought to understand nature and humans rationally rather than through religion and myth. The major fields of science, including biology, geology, and physics, emerged during the industrial period. So did the field of sociology. Named by Auguste Comte, this social science concentrated on the nature of human society and human relationships. Early sociologists were immersed in observing the forms of social, economic, and religious life that had arisen with industrialism, and contrasting them with the traditional forms of life that had once held sway in Europe and elsewhere. The writings of these social scientists depict the emergence of a modern world regulated by rationality and rational order and the decline of a traditional world ruled by custom and myth.

Sociology and Religion

The work of sociologists today is still underpinned by the social science theories developed during the industrial period. These complex and related theories were about secularization, pluralism, individualism, urbanism, and alienation, among many other things. In many of these theories religion was an important issue. The basic thrust of secularization theory, for example, was that in a modern world, religion was imperiled. One major strand of thought about secularization said that religion would eventually lose credence and become so generalized as to be valueless to the practical needs of individuals. Another major strand of thought about secularization said that changes in the structure of society would bring about the demise of institutional religion. As modern society developed, religion would be driven from the public realm. Religion would be confined to the private lives of individuals.

Sociologists often failed to depict concretely the forces that were to bring about the demise of religion. In fact, until even recently, scholars tended to paint these forces as dark and mysterious. Disturbingly, social scientists also accepted virtually as tenets a number of early sociological theories about modernity and religion. Secularization theory is a prime example. Some theories also were never properly tested by the type of extended and careful research demanded by the scientific process. On occasion, when empirical evidence that contradicted these theories arose, a number of scholars simply ignored the evidence or dismissed it outright.

Modern ideas about secularization are usually based on the supposed effects of pluralism and individualism. In recent decades, the intellectual driving force in the United States behind the theory that society was becoming secularized was Peter L. Berger. An influential Austrian-born sociologist at Boston University, Berger set forth a revised theory of secularization in the 1960s in his book *The Sacred Canopy*. In that book, he placed the blame for secularization on pluralism. In an increasingly pluralistic society, people are faced with contending religious views. The fact that other religious views exist reduces the ability of a religious body and its believers to claim long-held religious creeds as exclusively true. Pluralism thus strips religious groups and their beliefs of *plausibility*. "The pluralistic situation . . . makes it ever more difficult to maintain or to construct anew viable plausibility structures for religion," he said in the book's conclusion. Collapsing around us then with the development of pluralism, as Berger described it, is the protective structure of common conviction, a sacred canopy that shelters society and people from the menace of meaninglessness (Berger 1969).

The Crumpling of Older Theory

In the decades following the publication of Berger's *The Sacred Canopy*, it became clear to many scholars that the facts of American life did not fit his theory. He had written the book at the time when the memberships of mainline denominations had dropped precipitously, which to many people was sure proof of secularization. But in the years after his book was published, evangelicalism and fundamentalism powerfully came into their own in the United States. Along with Pentecostal bodies, these movements attracted many adherents, and they became socially and politically influential among Americans. Indeed, Dean Kelley, who despite being a liberal Methodist pastor and longtime official of the ecumenical National Churches of Christ, firmly asserted in a controversial book, *Why Conservative Churches Are Growing*, that by sticking with demanding beliefs and by policing the rules, churches could buck the forces of modernity and prosper (Kelley 1972). In several articles and books, James D. Hunter, a University of Virginia sociologist suggested, too, that yes it was possible to buck modernism, if a religious group was sheltered from pluralism. That religious group either could be found in a place that changed slowly, such as a rural town, or that drew its adherents from those whom pluralism touched least—socially and economically disadvantaged people. The statistical picture that Hunter presented of Protestant conservatives was of people who were much poorer and less educated than liberal Protestants and whose jobs were less desirable than those of their liberal Protestant counterparts (Hunter 1983).

As some social scientists pondered the resurgence of conservative religion, other scholars focused on the troubles of mainline churches. These latter scholars, picking up on the essence of Kelley's assertions, placed the blame for the decline of mainline membership in the 1960s squarely at the door of mainline churches themselves. Because of growing pluralism and individualism, they said, mainline churches had been forced to relax religious strictures. As a result, people had drifted away from mainline churches, usually to embrace no religion. Mainline churches had forfeited their hold on people. That was the conclusion of *Vanishing Boundaries*, for example, written by a trio of sociologists who had studied what had happened to Presbyterian confirmands in their later years (Hoge, Johnson, and Luidens 1994). This same message was generally reflected in other substantive studies, including *American Mainline Religion* by Wade Clark Roof, a sociologist at the University of California, Santa Barbara, and William McKinney, who was then a sociologist at Hartford Seminary (Roof and McKinney 1989). Roof delved deeper into the role of individualism in *A Generation of Seekers*, a study of Baby Boomers whose changed religious attitudes and patterns of participation he and McKinney had earlier identified as a central cause of mainline demise (Roof 1993).

From Individualism to Sheilaism

This line of thought about the impact of individualism was similarly reflected in *Religion and Personal Autonomy* by Phillip E. Hammond (Hammond 1992). Individualism was an aspect of modern society caused by people turning from institutional mandates (like those of churches). Authors like Hammond said that growing individualism had shifted the foundation of church participation from obligatory to voluntary, and that had loosened the personal commitment of people to churches. Instead of being set in a particular religion from birth, people now made choices about religion. Other scholars pushed these ideas about the role of religious individualism further and raised the specter that religious bodies themselves were becoming irrelevant. Robert N. Bellah and colleagues, in their study of religious individualism in America, *Habits of the Heart*, told the now well-known story of Sheila, one of their interviewees, whose faith "somehow seems a perfectly natural expression of current American religious life." A nurse, Sheila had put together her own religion independent of any church, an institution whose services she rarely attended: "It's Sheilaism. Just my own little voice" (Bellah et al. 1986).

But Sheila turned out not to be the iconoclastic portrait of contemporary religion for sociologists of religion, though many examples of Sheilaism could be spotted by researchers. For tens of millions of Americans, religious bodies remain important and relevant places in their lives. Evangelicals, fundamentalists, and Pentecostals also turned out not to be mere backwoods zealots. Reliable national surveys noted that these movements were not consigned only to the places and people where pluralism was weakest. In fact, adherents of these religiously conservative movements were increasingly part of mainstream American life. Furthermore, despite Kelley's claim that strict churches were more appealing, another sociologist, Joseph B. Tamney, contended that people are not enchanted with rule-bound bodies. His intensive study of churches and religion in Muncie, Indiana, found Muncie residents preferred churches to be open and tolerant (Tamney and Johnson 1998; Tamney 2002, Tamney et al. 2003). Meanwhile, membership losses began to level off in mainline churches, down to shedding a few thousand adherents a year, according to their annual reports. As we see later, sociologists now say that declining birth rates and changes in marriage have more to do with mainline decline than changing strictures (Hout, Greeley, and Wilde 2001).

A New Paradigm

In a pivotal article published in a scholarly journal in 1993, R. Stephen Warner, a sociologist of religion at the University of Illinois at Chicago, challenged the mindset that governed how scholars studied churches and religion in the United States and offered a new paradigm in the sociology of religion. Aiming directly at Berger's pluralism thesis, he noted that despite the nation's increasing diversity, the United States had not become a less vital place for religion and religious organizations (Warner 1993).

Warner's article went on to dispute ideas about pluralism and its effect on religion that then reigned in the social sciences. His article was pivotal, too, because having challenged the scholarly mindset, the article helped to marshal a wave of academic interest in religion and religious communities among younger scholars. The supposed demise of religion had meant that religion was not a subject worthy of sustained academic interest. After all, religion would eventually disappear. Other than writing sweeping essays on American religion, the startling truth was that few sociologists had actually engaged in the intimate study of religious congregations and the role of religion in the everyday lives of Americans. Based on what the theories said, and not on research, sociologists had assumed that religious congregations were places of trivialized faith and that religion among individuals had turned private and its impact on broader public concerns had diminished.

Two examples of this assumption are *The Suburban Captivity of the Churches* by Gibson Winter, a Chicago Theological School professor, and Peter L. Berger's *The Noise of Solemn Assemblies*, both published in 1961. Winter, an Episcopal priest, even claimed that the continued preservation of congregations as the basis of the Christian church was "doomed to failure" (Winter 1961). Neither book involved fieldwork among congregations but was based purely on social science theory and on the subjective observations of the authors. Even so, these two works, and others like them published later, have clouded how many generations of pastors, religious officials, and seminary teachers viewed churches, and fed a continuing illusion—a priori—that local congregations were ill, troubled, or just plain out of it.[1] It has created a common wisdom about congregations that persists today.

Competitive Religion

In his article, Warner also called attention to a group of scholars who at the time were radically suggesting that instead of pluralism reducing religious activity, pluralism encouraged religious activity. This "rational choice" theory is based on supply-side economic models.[2] Led by Rodney Stark, Roger Finke, and Laurence Iannaccone, these economists and sociologists aggressively pushed the idea that religious bodies operated in a religious market. Entrepreneurial church bodies with the strongest religious message (or product) and determined evangelism (or marketing) captured the most religious members (or consumers), who paid for the product handsomely with high commitment. Successful religions had a strong product. "Humans want their religion to be sufficiently potent, vivid, and compelling so that it can offer them rewards of great magnitude" (Finke and Stark 1992).

Drawing on their analysis of U.S. church membership over the past two centuries, Finke and Stark argued in their book, *The Churching of America 1776–1990*, that in time of religious monopoly, as was the case in parts of colonial America, religion did not thrive. But when the religious marketplace was opened to competition, as happened during the religious awakenings in the new American republic, religion flourished and church membership spread. This radical contention of "rational choice" scholars that pluralism fostered robust religion ran into numerous analytical complications when it was subjected to statistical studies. These complications required "rational choice" proponents to clarify their assumptions several times. Nevertheless, the research on "rational choice" theory has provided interesting evidence to sociologists that though sometimes pluralism is not so good for religion, sometimes religion does benefit from pluralism (Chaves and Gorski 2001).

A Sociological Revelation

Moreover, Warner's pivotal 1993 article helped launch a number of careful congregational studies by sociologists. Among the first sociologists to have intimately investigated a congregation was Warner himself. Published before his pivotal article, his *New Wine in Old Wineskins* was among the first such research, too, to sense that the prevailing sociological notions about the religious life of congregations and individuals had missed the target (Warner 1990).[3] More dramatically, after a study of several middle-class, white congregations around Oak Park, Illinois, Penny Edgell said the study suggested that "the standard narrative [of sociology] needs to be reworked." These congregations of "individualistic, cosmopolitan professionals" did not match the theoretical expectations of pluralism. A University of Minnesota sociologist, Edgell said that, in fact, "voluntarism and pluralism can lead to religious and civic vitality" (Becker 1999).

What she found in congregations has been repeatedly uncovered by other sociologists studying religious communities. These studies also challenged the contention that the commitment of people to congregations was weakened in a pluralistic and individualistic world and that congregations have become places of out-of-it privatized religion.

A study of congregations in an exurban Atlanta community found that newer residents were able to manage a complex tangle of ties to religious and civic bodies, ties that were robust and fulfilling (Eiesland 2000). Speaking of the voluntary nature of present-day church membership, another scholar says flatly in her own nationwide study of congregations, "The substance and depth of these commitments are no less real simply because an individual is committed to other institutions, or because the commitment may not last a lifetime" (Ammerman 1997a). In numerous different surveys, too, Americans also claim to be highly satisfied with their congregations (Gallup 1990; Woolever and Bruce 2002), including among younger generations (Carroll and Roof 2002). Unlike the dire predictions of Winter and others, the accumulated evidence from these congregational studies is that local congregations are durable institutions and that they provide people with important religious space (Marty 1998).

The Arrival of Postmodern Theory and Religion

A number of major new social and economic situations arose by the middle of the twentieth century that led to changes in scholarly concepts of society. Many of these new concepts were readily adopted within religious circles and integrated into congregational literature. The new situations included the expansion of consumerism, the emergence of mass media, and the dawn of globalization. Instead of focusing on the manufacture of capital goods such as steel and locomotives, as was the case in the nineteenth century, industries shifted to producing consumer products. Cars and televisions now rolled along assembly lines. The advent of television launched a media that could simultaneously and immediately reach virtually every person. About 600 million people worldwide watched *Apollo 11* depart for the moon, carrying the first humans who were to land there on July 20, 1969. Like the media, the economy, too, was slipping over national boundaries. Products were increasingly made in other parts of the world and imported into the old industrial countries. New cars arrived in the United States from Japan. In a short time, car imports from Japan went from 0 to 2.3 million vehicles a year. Other important new social situations included the transformation of women's status, as well as novel changes in family structure and in sexual relationships. With the emergence of these new social and economic situations, social scientists referred to the new time as "postmodern." Tinkering with older sociological theories to reconcile them to new situations, as well as to resolve a number of problems associated with the old theories, academics also began to label the newer social science propositions as postmodern.[4]

The Postmodern Evolution

Postmodern theories are not unlike modern theories. They focus on changes caused by pluralism, for example, because pluralism increasingly shapes our globalizing society. Other changes they highlight are the decline of tradition (detraditionalization), the evolution of even greater individualism (radical individualism), and the devaluation of science and rationality (alternative rationality). Postmodern theories have been important in explaining such social phenomena as the changing status of women in the workplace and at home, the place of power in social relations, the dynamics of new religious movements, and the reshaping of attitudes toward sexual activity and orientation.

The evolution of postmodern theories has also been influenced by the collapse of key modernist theories, like those on secularization. Old modernist theory had foreseen the demise of religion in society and among individuals. But religion was not extinguished. As it turned out, secularization theory was at best shaky. Scholars had once thought, for example, that the United States would eventually become secularized like Europe a century ago. Particularly among European scholars, Europe was thought to the model of what would happen to religion in a modern society. Now, instead of seeing Europe as the epitome of modernity and secularization, some European scholars say the continent where secularization theory was born is not in fact a good example of religious change in the modern, or postmodern, world (Davie 2000; Davie 2002). Though a few scholars earnestly continue to defend variants of the theory, secularization theory is considered dead in many sociological circles. However, the view that the United States is a secularizing society still oddly persists among some religious leaders and theologians.

Rethinking Religion

Faced with the persistence of religion, social scientists have reworked theories about religion, pluralism, and individualism. Notably, Berger, faced with the overwhelming evidence that religion and society was not taking the course he had said it would, publicly retreated from his original proposition about pluralism. He declared in a 1998 *Christian Century* article, "Most of the world today is as religious as it ever was and, in a good many locales, more religious than ever" (Berger 1998). In the same

Christian Century article, Berger outlined his revised theory as follows.

"People may still hold the same beliefs and values that were held by their predecessors . . . but they will hold them in a different manner. . . . Pluralism brings on an era of many choices and, by the same token, an era of uncertainty."

Instead of pluralism *imperiling* religion, pluralism creates particular *changes* in religion. Pluralism increases religious anxiety and promotes religious choice. The resulting changes in religion and religious belief can be summarized in three points.

- The emphasis is on personal spirituality over institutional religiousness. People are religious seekers who are not confined to the religion in which they are born.

- People use a "cafeteria" approach to developing religious beliefs. Fed by an expanding popular religious media—an actual religious market—they pick up religious ideas from a variety of places. An example of the cafeteria approach is the popularity of Thomas Merton, a Catholic convert and Trappist monk, who blended Catholic spirituality with Buddhist precepts and Native American mysticism.[5] Examples of a religious market abound. Take, for example, the events listing in an alternative weekly in Asheville, North Carolina. It includes dozens of local religious activities ranging from daily meditative Hindu satsangs to Edgar Cayce spiritualist seminars. Appearing in *The New York Times* hardcover bestseller list for self-help books in spring 2003 was a book on purposeful living written by the pastor of a Baptist megachurch in California. On a Spanish cable channel are ads selling CDs of popular new evangelical worship hymns. The number of religious Web sites on the Internet is now staggering.

- People have turned away from religious tradition. Congregations that have sprung up in recent decades have abandoned traditional symbols and language of the church. New paradigm churches and seeker churches lack stained glass and crosses (Miller 1997; Sargeant 2000).

Spiritual Searching

The scholar whose work is most attuned to postmodern concepts, and one of the scholars whose work is often written for religious institutions and its leaders, is Wade Clark Roof, a University of California at Santa

Barbara sociologist. Agreeing with Berger's newer contentions about the effects of pluralism, Roof says people today are on a "spiritual quest." Shorn of the certainties imbedded into the religion of the past, they are forced to reflect about religion. This reflective spirituality lies beyond the bounds of religious institutions; it is turned deeply inward. What matters is not the religious body and its ways of believing and doing but "the inner life and its cultivation" (Roof 1999).

Instead of Bellah's Sheila, Roof gives us Vicki. Browsing around for a religion, Vicki Feinstein is a Boston physical therapist who has experimented with Scientology, read about Buddhism, dabbled in spiritual healing, and wonders if *Star Trek* could be considered a religion. (The characters "all get along well and look to a future together. It's promising. If we lived that way we would have a better world.") Vicki Feinstein is among the four portraits of religious questors described by Roof in *Spiritual Marketplace*. The other questors he describes are Karen Potter, a Southern Baptist who has taken "a leave of absence" from church to explore feminist spirituality; Sam Wong, a second-generation Chinese American computer programmer who with his wife has hooked up with the Vineyard Fellowship; and Sara Caughman, a 40-ish graphic designer who after years of being unchurched, is active in an Episcopal parish accepting of diverse lifestyles. Notably, these portraits ring of radical individualism, antirationalism, and social fragmentation. In some fashion, too, each person has left the beaten path of religious tradition and now depends on his or her own celestial readings to plot their religious journey. But unlike Sheila, who made up her religion, Vicki is a shopper hunting the right religious product. Notes Roof, "It is not that the world has gone secular, lost all scripts of embedding the secular; instead, the world has become a gigantic maze of alternative paths requiring of individuals a level of decision-making and accountability on scale unlike anything previous Americans have known—and involving in a most fundamental way, things of the spirit." Echoing similar themes are Robert Wuthnow in *After Heaven,* and Amanda Porterfield, a University of Wyoming religion professor, in *The Transformation of American Religion* (Wuthnow 1998; Porterfield 2001).

Problems with Postmodern Religion

As with earlier theories about secularization and pluralism, doubts are emerging among scholars about postmodern conceptions of religion. First, the portrayals of postmodern believers by Roof and other scholars are not inaccurate. But the evidence is that these portraits apply to only a *fraction* of religious believers. Roof's Vicki is not an ordinary person; her story is exceptional. Peculiar as she might seem to many people, to Roof, Vicki Feinstein has the potential to become "the icon of the age," though to what extent, he admits, is unknown. Perhaps not at all. Roof notes that the amorphous collection of religious believers in which Vicki belongs makes up only about one in seven Americans, using the broadest possible definitions of that group. This focus on the exceptional by postmodern scholars is like looking at society through an immobile telescope. We are transfixed by stunning detail, but what we see is only a fixed piece of the landscape. We miss the actual rich variety that exists in the broader landscape.

How Much Change?

Besides challenging the postmodern emphasis on the exceptional, some scholars are also raising questions about the actual degree of religious change. If religion is changing, then people's religious attitudes, beliefs, and practices should change steadily across time. These religious changes would be found in surveys conducted in different years, and among successive generations. But the survey evidence is increasingly showing that while social and religious differences between the present time and that of 50 years ago are remarkable, social and religious changes in recent years are close to insignificant. Indeed, in the Gallup Surveys, which provide a glimpse into religious beliefs and practices over the past half century, the percentage of Gallup respondents who said they attended church or synagogue over the past week, or who claimed to be part of a church or synagogue, has not changed significantly over the past two decades. This steadying of churchgoing and membership comes after a significant decline in those activities in the 1960s. Also, the percentage of Gallup respondents who say that religion is not very important in their lives peaked at about one-eighth of respondents about two decades ago and has not changed much since (Healy 1999). Of course, postmodern scholars are not claiming that religion is being diminished, but that it is being changed.

An item that scholars single out as evidence of religious change is the number of people who agree in surveys that one can be a good Christian or Jew without attending church or synagogue. To sociologists, a positive reply smacks of religious individualism. The less people depend on institutions, the more individualistic they have become. In their book on mainline religion, Roof and McKinney say that a positive answer means that "religious authority lies in the believer—not in the church, not in the Bible . . ." In 1978, 78 percent of Gallup Poll respondents said that one could be a good Christian or Jew even if you failed to attend worship. Replying to the same question, 76 percent of Gallup respondents answered positively in 1988 (Gallup 1988). Roof asked a similar question in a four-state survey conducted in 1988–1989 among Baby Boomers and pre-Boomers for *A Generation of Seekers*. In that survey, about two-thirds of the respondents said that attendance does not make for a good Christian or Jew. In a 1997 survey of Catholic confirmands in later life, 64 percent agreed that a person could be a good Catholic without going to Mass (Hoge et al. 2001). The highly respected General Social Survey (GSS) asked a question in its 1988–1991 and 1998 surveys that was different from Gallup's. More of the GSS respondents said that it was important to attend religious services regularly in order to be a good Christian or a Jew than said it was unimportant. The results were virtually no different between the 1998 and 1988–1991 surveys. (More interestingly, in a related GSS question, a majority of respondents agreed it was highly important to follow the teachings of their church or synagogue in order to be a good Christian or Jew.)[6] While the better known Gallup Poll and the other survey data support the idea of pervasive religious individualism, the more trusted GSS data does not. But most important, neither the Gallup nor the GSS data offers convincing evidence that religious individualism, as measured by this question, has significantly increased over the past 25 years.

Overplaying Generational Change

Another place that the progressive effects of postmodern trends could be expected to show up is among successive generations. And in fact, gaps in attitudes and practices do exist between generations. But the big gap in religious attitudes and practices is largely between the group of people born in the two decades after 1945—Baby Boomers—and the group born in the decades before World War II—pre-Boomers. If religious changes have transpired continuously over time, then the generations that followed the Baby Boomers should have experienced significant changes, too. Despite popular notions otherwise, significant changes are not apparent between Boomers and their successors, GenXers. In an attempt to understand generational changes in congregations, Jackson W. Carroll, a religious scholar at Duke University, and Roof surveyed generational groups in North Carolina and southern California (Carroll and Roof 2002). Unlike the wide divide in attitudes and practices they and many others have found between Boomers and pre-Boomers, the division between Boomers and GenXers is narrow. Mainline Boomers and GenXers are involved in religious institutions at nearly the same rate, for example. Between Boomers and pre-Boomers, the gap in attendance is a chasm: pre-Boomers attend much more often. Also, GenXers are as attached to their religious congregations as Boomers, but Boomers are much less attached than pre-Boomers. In fact, Carroll and Roof say that the religious differences that exist between Boomers and GenXers may have more to do with their respective stage in life than generational culture. Notably, a study of recent Catholic confirmands found no substantial differences in religious attitudes between Boomers and GenXers (Hoge et al. 2001). A telling academic article recently noted, too, that despite claims among popular religious writers of growing religious alienation among younger generations, the proportion of American youth estranged from organized religion is small, and furthermore, that proportion has not changed in recent decades (Smith et al. 2003).[7]

Not-So-Radical Individualism

Based on replies to questions including the one about being a good Christian or Jew, scholars are also contesting postmodern notions of radical individualism. In measuring the extent of individualism, social scientists have depended on responses to key survey questions, including the survey question discussed previously. For example, Carroll and Roof found, based on a statistical scale, that individualism had risen both between pre-Boomers and Boomers, and between Boomers and GenXers.[8] However, a number of scholars have pointed out that survey responses are being misread to say that people are willingly becoming more individualistic. Instead, these scholars say the responses really show that people increasingly understand that in present-day society, *choices can be made.* Furthermore, these scholars note that when given religious choices, most people stick to the religious faith of their parents, and when they do deviate, they select a faith basically like the religion or denomination in which they were raised. Switching between religious denominations rose in the 1960s and 1970s but has not grown in recent years. Moreover, when people do jump ship, they usually leap to a denomination that is theologically similar to the one they just left, according to several statistical studies of religious affiliation. Religious liberals usually stay religious liberals. Religious conservatives usually stay religious conservatives. Instead of indicating that people are becoming radically individualistic and straying religiously, the survey data is showing that people stay close to the religion of their birth. (An exception to this finding is switching to nonaffiliation, which is growing but is infrequent.) What this data shows is that unlike people a few generations ago, people today are acknowledging that, if they had wished, they could have picked something else. And yet, they didn't (Sherkat 2001; Bibby 1999; and Hadaway and Marler 1993).

Tradition Lives On

Other postmodern scholars' contentions are also under dispute, including contentions about tradition. Notably, despite the postmodern emphasis on loss of tradition, tradition persists even in unlikely religious settings today. Hundreds of evangelicals led by Peter E. Gillquist, a Campus Crusade for Christ official, joined the ritual-laden Antiochian Orthodox Church in 1987, a flow toward traditionalism by numerous evangelicals that continues today. In once rural Forsyth County outside of Atlanta, a new Orthodox Christian church in the now rapidly growing suburb posts on its Web site stories of conversions to Orthodox Christianity by Protestants. Journalist Colleen Carroll documents cases of young Catholics, enthused with evangelicalism, staying put in the Catholic Church because the young Catholics are more moved by ritual than they are by the spontaneous and unconventional services of Protestant evangelical churches (Carroll 2002). Often to please the young, Reformed synagogues have reinstated prayers in Hebrew and returned to rituals dropped by earlier generations, as a number of reports and studies on changes in synagogue life have documented. In fact, one religious scholar, Dorothy C. Bass of Valparaiso University, argues that tradition is intrinsic to religious congregations. Tradition provides a congregation with the tools it needs in order to engage the world (Bass 1998).

Postmodern theory on religion has flaws. The events scholars cite as evidence of postmodern change tend to be exceptional rather than ordinary. The empirical evidence is growing that despite how much attitudes, beliefs, and participation changed several decades ago, religious and social changes have become muted in recent years. Clear differences are not evident between new generations. Pluralism and individualism have not created the pervasive, continuing change in religion that postmodern theory has suggested should be occurring. Tradition even persists in the most unlikely places. In fact, as I show in chapter 3, tradition has an essential function in postindustrial society. Unfortunately, the collapse of the old theories and the problems with postmodern theory also undermine much of the current thinking in religious circles about religion and congregations, thinking that also persists as conventional wisdom in the bulk of the congregational literature. The problems with that self-help literature, as I show in the next section, extend beyond having outdated information to the nature of the literature itself.

The Congregational Self-Help Market

Today virtually every major religious publisher has an expansive list of books devoted to congregations. How to lead them. How to grow them. How to change them. Numerous for-profit and nonprofit firms sell videos, training programs, and other similar tools to help religious leaders and congregants achieve specific objectives, whether building membership, raising money, or revitalizing worship. Mixed with long-established, reputable organizations marketing traditional products are individuals and groups that have recently sprung up with a Web site and an inclination to a certain ministry. The religious marketplace that has grown up for congregational self-help resources rivals the growing market for personal religious and spiritual books, Web sites, DVDs, and other media for individuals. No statistics exist to quantify this congregational self-help market, but it is safe to assume that nearly every religious leader and congregation has used such resources in one way or another. Also lacking is a rigorous critical evaluation of the material, and the material has a number of faults. Not the least of those faults is that much of these resources reinforce a conventional wisdom about religion and congregations that is contrary to what has emerged in recent studies by sociologists of religion and others.[9]

The Nature of the Material

The congregational material falls into two genres. The works of independent consultants, denominational advisors, and many others who are interested in the practical aspects of congregations make up the first genre. This literature usually stresses how to make a congregation grow and overcome obstacles to that growth. To that end, the authors are mainly interested in practical results. The second genre is theologically based material. Clergy and seminary professors are often the authors. They are usually interested in conceptualizing how a religious community ought to be ideally. Those authors seek what, in a sense, rings true religiously. The first genre applies personal learning and experience; the second appeals to theological perspectives and interpretations. These starting points shape how the authors perceive religious communities and the world around those bodies. Unfortunately, the first genre is sometimes too quick to accept explanations of social and religious trends, no matter how shaky, if the explanations seem to fit the genre's preconceptions of congregations and the world. The second genre often sees congregations and the world through the lens of theology, which leads to assumptions and conclusions that do not necessarily match life as it is actually really lived. More often than not, both genres embrace the conventional wisdom of religious demise and decline and that congregations are inherently "out of it." That conventional wisdom seems to persist within religious circles because now both mainline and evangelical seminaries inoculate students with that view (Carroll et al. 1997).

How the Genres Shape Perception

Two books that illustrate the respective genres are *Discontinuity and Hope* by Lyle E. Schaller and *Resident Aliens: Life in the Christian Colony* by Stanley Hauerwas and William H. Willimon. Schaller has been a prolific writer of congregational self-help books. Hauerwas and Willimon were chaplain and professor at Duke University and Duke Divinity School, respectively. These books are not selected as illustrations because they are bad. They are selected because they are known and good versions of the two genres of congregational literature.[10] These works are heartfelt and thoughtful efforts to address the problems of congregations as the authors see those problems. The authors worked with the knowledge at hand, which as it turns out, was flawed. The point here is how each genre shapes perception and why the congregational material needs to move beyond those perceptions. Schaller's book is an attempt to harvest decades of consultative wisdom into a broad vision at the start of a new century. Hauerwas and Willimon are trying to inspire, if not enlighten, pastors struggling to put a solid theological base to their ministry. Both books are directed more toward Protestant mainline bodies than to other bodies, but not strictly so.

Feeding on Anxiety

Stated in his standard point-by-point, matter-of-fact style, Schaller's premise is simple. The congregations that will succeed this century are those that resolve to be competitive, become large, set high expectations, offer a variety of wide-reaching ministries, and run themselves through lay ministry teams (Schaller 1999). These qualities are indeed admirable attributes useful to good congregational ministry. Schaller also contends that congregations that are middle-sized or rooted in European tradi- tions and do not adopt "American-made" innovations in theology, wor- ship, and management are in trouble. (Small, caring fellowships are exceptions.) Assembling lines upon lines of information about social and religious changes, some incorrect or misstated and often lacking attri- bution, Schaller tells his readers that these facts are evidence that con- gregations must change. Here is the first problem with this book, a fault intrinsic to the genre: it builds anxiety. Schaller states tersely at one point, "Deny this has happened." The book's second fault is common to this genre: narrowness. Schaller has a high criterion of what constitutes suc- cess in a congregation because he is apparently instilled with false fears of religious demise. He gives advice as a result that is focused toward a few favored types of congregational models because those types of con- gregations appear to produce the most membership growth. Schaller's eye is sharp. Much of his advice is practical, if not sage. But curiously, his eye has failed to encompass the breadth and depth of religious prac- tice that now characterizes the American religious landscape, including in his own hometown of Naperville, a study of which appears in a later chapter. Anxiety and narrowness do not encourage the critical thinking that is needed today to understand what a congregation is about and what ministry and mission is appropriate to its place and time. In build- ing a case for radical change, the genre raises anxiety among the reli- gious faithful as a means to force an agenda that in the end may not be helpful to a religious body. Anxiety breeds institutional isomorphism— doing what others have done based on the conventional wisdom cur- rent among other leaders in religious institutions and ministry rather than studying carefully their own situation and the real religious needs of their own community (DiMaggio and Powell 1983).

Missing the Reality

The second book, that of Hauerwas and Willimon, is theologically driven. As is common to both genres, the emphasis is on what congregations are doing wrong. But the theological basis of this genre, and of this book, places stress more on how society has gone bad. Congregations must restore society to proper ways of thinking and being (Hauerwas and Willimon 1989). Unlike Schaller, who says religious bodies have failed to change with the world, Hauerwas and Willimon are critical of how religious bodies *have changed* to accommodate the world. Instead of Schaller's *transformed* church, the authors want a *transforming* church. Their premise is that the world around the church is no longer the Christian society that has been the foundation of Western civilization since Emperor Constantine, a Christian convert, ruled a diminished Roman Empire. That society has died. Anecdotally to the authors, that society died when the theater in the authors' Bible Belt hometown of Greenville, South Carolina, decided in 1963 to show movies on Sundays. Now consumerism and individualism are rampant in society. In response, the authors call on congregations and religious leaders to ask hard questions and turn "adventuresome" in their ministry.

Two faults common to the genre are illustrated in the book. The first problem is that the theological perspective creates a view of society that is sometimes out of touch with the lived reality: ever sinful, people have gone consumer mad. They are possessed of unbounded individualism or have devolved into postmodern relativists. In one section, Hauerwas and Willimon tell of a church member who fought a pastor's idea of starting a community daycare center. The idea was interpreted by the church member as giving in to career-driven couples who dump their children on others as they overwork to buy more consumer goods—a case of theological truth-telling, the authors say. Despite the theological view, the reality today is that many middle-income couples are both at work because the postindustrial economy, with its growing wage disparity, has driven both marital partners into the workplace. The second fault in this genre is in the remedy, especially for mainline bodies. The remedy in this book is to pull people into tight religious communities that counteract the world around them. But the fact is, especially in mainline bodies, that congregants have wide social networks that are needed for their well-being and the conduct of their lives. To achieve such an ideal congregation, those networks would have to be closed up. Congregants would have to abandon relatives, friends, and colleagues.

Concerns Over the Material

Because the congregational self-help material has become such an enormous industry, the material has taken on a sense of legitimacy that is sometimes undeserved. The reason that the material is so dependent on the conventional wisdom to the point that it ignores sociological developments, or that it selects only developments that fit within that wisdom, is because each genre is restricted in how it sees the world, whether through its own preconceptions or through a theological lens. More alarmingly, the material sometimes utilizes pseudosociological studies that lack competence and merit. The situation with this material is such that in one academic article reviewing research on youth and religion, the authors bemoaned the "journalistic, impressionistic, or semi-autobiographical" nature of popular material on youth religion. As the authors note:

> [T]hese books are being consumed by tens if not hundreds of thousands of parents, youth ministers, church pastors, denominational leaders, journalists, teachers, and others in the reading public. This, in turn, is helping to form a socially constructed reality that may or may not actually comport with what we might know to be closer to the actual empirical truth. And this may have consequences in forming (and perhaps reproducing self-fulfilling prophesy) parental expectations, youth self-images, and the resource allocations of religious organizations. (Smith, Faris, and Denton 2003)

The authors, who are sociologists of religion, echo the concerns of other social scientists who care deeply about religious institutions. But it is not the responsibility of sociologists to rid the religious marketplace of pseudoscience. The primary responsibility of scholars is to the advancement of scientific understanding in their discipline. The onus is on the religious community to be more aware of the real state of religion in America. The religious community needs to look more critically, too, at the material being produced in the congregational self-help market.

Turning to a Different Explanation

Postmodern theory has not gotten religion right. But turning to a postindustrial explanation offers a better and fuller understanding of what has happened to religion. That explanation begins with the fundamental changes that have transpired in the U.S. and world economy in recent decades. Those changes have shaken the social foundations of the old industrial nations of Europe, America, and elsewhere. Those changes have reverberated through society, people, and institutions, disordering the social landscape.

This postindustrial transformation has changed religion and reconfigured religious institutions in ways that are often different than postmodern theory has contended. Unlike postmodern theory, with its focus on growing individualism, vanishing tradition, and dissolving rationality, a postindustrial perspective focuses on the actual story of how people have been deprived of the social foundations on which they once have stood and that they now seek to rebuild. In this postindustrial perspective, many of the events of contemporary life spotlighted by postmodern scholars are also being highlighted. But the postindustrial perspective sees these events moving differently than postmodern theory. Indeed, in the postindustrial narrative, present-day individuals are understood to be intuitively reestablishing themselves religiously and socially—rerooting. Significantly for religious bodies and their leaders, and despite the persistent, distorted view of congregations as bodies hapless in the face of change, religious communities play an important and vital role among people in postindustrial society. In fact, religious communities are being called to engage with people and society in new ways that are valuable and essential in this disordered postindustrial landscape.

Chapter 2

Change in Postindustrial America

Congregations are called to new roles as religious communities because the postindustrial transformation has disordered the social landscape. Earlier scholars thought the postindustrial transformation would brighten the lives of people, but instead postindustrialism has revealed a dark side. Turning the American dream into a nightmare for some people, the postindustrial emphasis on education has knocked out the middle rungs of the ladder of opportunity that once made it possible in industrial society for the diligent and hardworking to rise bit by bit in wages and job status—even if they had meager educations. Moreover, the postindustrial economy has created types of jobs that have led to a growing wage disparity between the uppermost and lowermost workers. The postindustrial transformation has brought changes that have weakened the old social classes, transformed work places, and reshaped physical places and social ties. Additionally, the postindustrial transformation has partly helped to maintain high rates of moving, to prolong the time of young adulthood, and to add more years to people's lives.

In short, these changes have disordered society, communities, and religious bodies. Indeed, the way we live, how we work, and what we value has profoundly changed. The previous chapter traced the religious changes of recent decades. In this chapter, I track the major economic and social changes of the postindustrial transformation, which are many, various, and related. More important, this chapter explores the economic and social reverberations of these changes and how these changes have transformed the place of religion in society and reconfigured religious communities into places where people reestablish their religious and cultural narratives. The first part of this chapter describes how the postindustrial transformation has changed society, and the second part describes how these changes have affected religion and congregations.

The Meaning of Postindustrialism

The postindustrial transformation is usually described as the contraction of manufacturing industries and the expansion of service employment. But the postindustrial transformation is more complicated than that description. The postindustrial transformation has occurred in what economists call the economically advanced nations. These advanced nations include the United States, the old industrial countries of Europe such as France, Germany, and Great Britain, and other places such as Japan. In these countries, old forms of manufacturing have declined since the 1960s and a new type of service economy has appeared. However, these countries have not lost all their manufacturing, just the industries that can easily produce goods at lower cost in emerging industrial countries such as China, South Korea, Malaysia, or Brazil. What is left in the old industrial countries are high-value products such as aircraft, specialty merchandise such as fashion wear, and low-value goods that are too bulky to ship cheaply, such as inexpensive washing machines. Jobs in manufacturing are less common now in economically advanced countries; however, the monetary value of products made in the old industrial countries has continued to rise because increasingly the goods produced are of higher value.[1]

The means of manufacturing in these advanced economies has changed, too. No longer needed are the types of mechanical skills that dominated industrial plants a few decades ago. Instead, technically trained employees run pristine factories where production lines are strung with robots and controlled by computers. But not all present-day manufacturing in the United States matches that description. Some manufacturing occurs in a growing "unofficial" economy, a designation given by economists to jobs which ignore legal regulations on wages, hours, and safety. In many American cities, fashion wear and even computer parts are assembled in piecework sweatshops or at home.

The Rise of Service Employment

Economists once thought that the service jobs, which now account for most employment in economically advanced nations, were peripheral to the economy. Now, economists see service jobs as the core of a global, postindustrial economy. What are service jobs and why have they become important? People in service jobs assist individuals and businesses, in contrast to manufacturing jobs, in which people are engaged in making actual goods. A doctor or a lawyer is engaged in services. So is the maid at a hotel or a clerk at a copy center. Sociologist Daniel Bell of Harvard University, whose work has been instrumental in understanding the postindustrial economy and society, describes three types of service industries. One type includes transportation and utility companies; a second type includes companies engaged in trade, finance, insurance, and real estate; and a third includes providers of health care, education, research, recreation, and governance (Bell 1999). Another scholar whose work has been influential is Saskia Sassen. A professor of sociology at the University of Chicago, she divides service industries into two groups. The first group, producer services, includes companies doing business with other companies (such as accounting firms), and the second, consumer services, consists of outfits basically taking care of individuals (such as a resort attraction in Florida). The first group enhances the value of corporations and their output; the second group of services essentially helps maintain the well-being of people (Sassen 2001).

Furthermore, Sassen describes a global economy in which postindustrial nations (and key global cities) are at its core. As the previous chapter mentioned, these economically advanced nations house thriving financial, managerial, and support systems that direct, equip, and facilitate a diverse and complex global economy. In these nations and cities, Sassen says, producer service companies employ legions of well-paid accountants, brokers, consultants, engineers, scientists, and other people in highly educated professions whose expertise enhances the work of large and intricate global corporations. In the global economy, the emerging industrial nations are now the producers of many goods, especially consumer products, because costs are low in those countries. Bell says what distinguishes postindustrialism is the importance of knowledge in the economy and the way that knowledge is being used. Sassen also points to rapid innovation as a defining element of the postindustrial economy, not only technological innovation with such developments as the personal computer and the Internet but also in more esoteric "knowledge" fields such as finance and organization (Sassen 2002).

The Postindustrial Predicament

The importance of knowledge and the emphasis on high-level "expert" services means that education is a necessity in the postindustrial economy. Quite simply, the jobs that pay well require lots of education. Left for people without suitable schooling are jobs that earn rock-bottom wages. The gap in income from top to bottom is staggering. In 2001, a person without a high school diploma earned an average of $18,793 a year. But a person holding a professional degree averaged $101,375, according to the U.S. Census Bureau. Growing income inequality is the postindustrial predicament. The path to a better job and a higher salary in the postindustrial job market *starts* with an extensive, quality education. In the old industrial economy, however, a worker with a high school diploma could, and often did, land a job at the local factory, learn the needed skills on the job, increase in pay, and climb the ranks through years of employment. The high school graduate could end up as a foreman—even run the factory. In the postindustrial economy, the way a high school graduate ends up as a manager today is by earning a college degree. That person still needs an MBA to advance beyond the lowest rungs of the corporate world. Indeed, without some postsecondary education, a high school graduate today may have trouble even landing a decent job.[2]

Wage Winners and Losers

In the postindustrial economy, occupations in the bottom tier are being pushed toward lower wages, while some occupations in the top tier— many of them in high-level producer service and technology fields— have seen sizable jumps in income. (But not all. Scholars note that doctors, university teachers, and some others who staff Bell's third type of service industry are also feeling pressure on their incomes.)[3] As Sassen claims, the disappearance of the industrial economy has voided an implicit contract between employers and employees: employers paid good wages so employees could buy what the company made. Often that wage—usually paid to a married male—was sufficient to support a family. But now, with goods made cheaply abroad, the incentive to pay good wages no longer exists. Instead, employers are under competitive pressure to cut wages. Sassen also contends that most jobs created by high-level producer service and technology sectors are low paying, not high paying. In data she reviews for New York City, for example, about 5 percent of workers in high-level sectors such as financial brokerages earned $100,000 or more a year, but over three-fifths of employees in those sectors were paid less than $40,000 a year. Instead of the postindustrial economy leading to the creation of many high-paying jobs, as many— including Bell—originally thought it would, Sassen says the postindustrial economy is actually generating many low-wage jobs. Moreover, a number of these low-wage jobs pay below subsistence levels (Sassen 2002).

Getting a clear picture of income inequality in the United States is difficult. Income inequality is also a sensitive political issue. However, many economists contend that, as a result of low-wage expansion, disparity is growing between the highest and lowest incomes. By its measures, the U.S. Census Bureau says that income disparity widened after 1967 until the early 1990s, when the economy began a long run of growth through 2001. Since then, income disparity has remained basically unchanged (DeNavas-Walt and Cleveland 2002). In its calculations, the Brookings Institution has also found that income disparity widened into the 1990s (Burtless 1999). The widening disparity is partly blamed on the apparent rapid expansion of the informal economy, where wages are often below the legal minimum. Notably, efforts to hike the minimum wage, which in real dollars was worth much less in 2002 than it was in 1968, have failed every year in Congress since 1995, when the minimum wage was last raised. Disparity is also becoming visible because people educated and trained in occupations that should land them a good salary are being pushed into lower wage jobs for which they are overtrained.[4] Helping to relieve some of the downward pressure on wages are changes since the 1960s in who goes to work in many U.S. households. The lone family breadwinner is a thing of the past. The full-time earnings of men have generally stagnated since 1970, but the full-time earnings of women have risen (DeNavas-Walt and Cleveland, 2002). The chief reason that household income has stayed relatively steady—with periodic upward and downward fluctuations—is that most married-couple households have two paychecks.

Archie Bunker and the End of an Era

A sociologist friend uses television's acrimonious Archie Bunker to explain to students the differences in wages between the industrial and postindustrial period. Archie is the lone breadwinner of his family. As poorly educated (and badly misinformed) as he was, Archie supported a wife, bought a home, and raised a daughter. Archie earned decent wages working on a loading dock. Later in the 1970s series, of course, Archie is hit by the industrial downturn. His plant closes, he loses his job, and he never again gets decent work.

Archie was a union man. Unions had fought lengthy and bitter struggles to secure Archie's decent wages. But these wages were not exorbitant; employers could afford to pay such wages in the late industrial period. The American dream was easier for many workers to realize then (excepting many minorities and women). In some minds, that time was a Golden Age. As one European sociologist says, "Postindustrial society may hold the promise of many wonders, but equality is probably not among them. Hence our growing nostalgia for the Golden Age" (Esping-Andersen 1999).

The Impact of Postindustrialism

As during the emergence of the industrial economy in nineteenth-century Europe, the advent of the postindustrial economy has had social reverberations. These reverberations have shaken up social class, the workplace, and urban geography. The postindustrial economy has contributed to a number of other developments, too. These developments include continual geographic mobility, delayed social maturity, and lengthening life expectancy. As we will see, these developments have not only affected people but also have contributed to a number of changes within religious bodies, both local and national.

The Fading of Social Class

A few decades ago, social scholars could easily depict what social class was. Class was a real attribute, a solid indicator of a person's social and economic status, whether high, low, or in between. Class governed how people ran their lives. Such is not clearly the case now. In recent years a debate has raged among scholars over whether class is still a valid way of measuring social and political traits. Some scholars—particularly postmodern scholars—have proclaimed that class as a social concept is dead. These debates among scholars are complex and often have more to do with definitions and theory than with how present-day society is stratified socially and economically.

In the industrial period, most of society was split into a white-collar middle class and a blue-collar laboring class. The middle class supplied the managers and clerks. The laboring class furnished factory workers and truck drivers. Both classes had distinct social and economic traits. In fact, the classes were often politically and culturally opposed to each other (Clark and Lipset 2001). Blue-collar unions and political clubs warred against the economic and political power of the middle class. Through its position in society, the middle class also had social clout. Middle-class values—and mainline religion—were upheld as the standard for the society. But the postindustrial transformation has obscured the once clear picture of class. The old class divisions have dissolved. People have become fuzzy about their class identity. Social class no longer governs the conduct of people as much as it once did, nor does social class bestow the clear sense of identity it once gave.

Redrawing the Class Categories

Although social class is no longer sure, one attribute we can still turn to is a person's occupation—whether he or she is a lawyer, technician, clerk, and so forth—as an indicator of that individual's social and economic situation. These occupational classes, however, are more a statistical category and are less a cohesive, value-laden social entity than were social classes. In recent decades, many scholars have pointed to the rise of the new professional class. Who is part of the new professional class is not entirely clear. Bell includes technicians, sales clerks, and others. Sassen restricts this occupational class to highly degreed and high-salaried professionals. Other scholars in recent decades have pointed to the emergence of deprived classes. William Julius Wilson, a well-regarded sociologist at Harvard University, describes the existence of a concentrated urban underclass. Calling its members the truly disadvantaged, Wilson says the underclass appeared because of the proliferation of dead-end low-wage service jobs, as well as inadequate schools, public indifference, and negligible community resources (Wilson 1987). One scholar of the postindustrial economy splits workers within the service industry into four occupational classes: professional, semiprofessional, skilled, and unskilled (Esping-Andersen 1993). In fact, most workers—whether in service industries or manufacturing—can be clustered into four basic occupational classes. As outlined below, these classes include the new professionals, service and technical workers, the working poor, and the desperately poor.

- At the top are the new professionals. Earning the highest incomes in the postindustrial economy, the new professionals are people with professional and graduate degrees. With jobs that are, of course, "professional," this group is usually employed by the specialized firms that have sprung up or expanded in recent times to help large corporations in such areas as accounting, law, finance, advertising, marketing, communications, consulting, and so on, as well as sometimes being directly employed by the corporations themselves. This group resembles the old upper middle-class. Indeed, a few scholars see the new professionals as simply a transformed upper-middle class.

- The services and technical group is the second and largest tier of postindustrial society. People in this amorphous group possess college degrees or have postsecondary schooling, such as associate degrees or technical certificates. People in this group usually work in semi- or nonprofessionalized jobs. They are clerical workers, sales-people, medical technicians, computer repair people, and others. This group includes technically trained workers in manufacturing, as well as workers whose jobs were once considered solidly profes-sional, such as primary school teachers. People employed in these types of jobs live modest but good lives. They own homes, drive cars, and buy consumer goods. But middling wages generally means two incomes are needed in the household. This group is generally composed of the descendants of the old laboring and lower middle classes, as well as people pushed out of the upper middle class.

- The working poor are the third tier of postindustrial society. Pos-sessing high school diplomas and sometimes postsecondary train-ing, the working poor labor in jobs—sometimes temporary or part-time—that require some skills. The working poor are near the bottom of the economic ladder. They lack the medical and retire-ment benefits generally available to the upper two tiers. They are laborers, convenience store clerks, cleaning people, and others. This class includes, for example, industrial workers in low-paying, low-skill jobs. Despite having jobs, many are impoverished or live pre-cariously above the poverty line. This group is made up of people whose ties are to the lower levels of the old laboring class.

- The bottom tier of postindustrial society is made up of the desper-ately poor. The desperately poor may lack high school diplomas and have few employable skills. When they get work, the pay is at the bottom of the legal scale, if not below it. They toil in fast-food chains, labor in off-the-book jobs. An unfortunately high propor-tion of this group is African American and increasingly Hispanic American. Until the 1990s, this group was concentrated in inner cit-ies. In the economically robust 1990s, the people in these desper-ately poor urban enclaves began to disperse around urban areas. Changes in federal urban policy also led to cities tearing down the public projects that once housed the desperately poor and replacing them with small, mixed-income developments.[5]

Thus are the changes in class. The ebbing of social classes has, of course, freed people from the oppressive restraints of social stratifica-tion, to the degree that it existed in the United States. But the ground on which cultural values, as well as religious faith, were once anchored has been eroded by the collapse of the old classes, too.

The Reshaping of Work

The old industrial economy emphasized orderly, routine systems of work; the new postindustrial economy values flexible and innovative approaches. Intensifying market competition and honest efforts by social scientists to enrich the workplace have driven these changes. The new approaches to work have resulted in greater organizational and worker flexibility, but scholars and workers alike are raising troubling questions about the effectiveness of these approaches and the effects these approaches have on people and society.

Employees today "are encountering genuinely new ways of producing and serving" (Smith 1997). The changes in work and among workers have come about because of an innovative, technological, and global postindustrial economy. Driving these changes is the need of businesses—especially manufacturing firms—to be ever more competitive, forcing an urgent search for more efficient forms of production. Also driving these changes are actual innovations in employment and organization that are based on a real desire to free workers from the mindless drudgery that dominated work in the old industrial economy. Behind each of these driving forces, too, is the feverish proliferating of new technologies, such as easy-to-use software and tireless industrial robots, that have boosted productivity, expanded skills, and sped communication.[6]

A Reward for Drudgery

Henry Ford's introduction of the assembly line in 1913 was an important development in the old industrial economy. The mass production of affordable goods—in Ford's case, the Model T—was made possible by the development of scientific management, a system for carefully controlling the efforts and time of each employee. Labeled "Fordism" by social scientists, this method of work organization permeated not only the nation's ever more prosperous factories, but increasingly, too, the growing offices of parent corporations that were being staffed with armies of clerks, typists, bookkeepers, and managers. Employees in these workplaces were ruled by a formidable hierarchy, performed tasks that were highly defined, and engaged in utterly repetitive routines. Management and labor were clearly different. In a nutshell, management thought and labor toiled. As a reward for toiling in such drudgery, labor earned decent wages with which to buy homes, cars, and consumer goods.

The downside of this system was its psychological and emotional toll. Social scientists found that workers were dissatisfied, bored, alienated, and lacked self-esteem. Nor did everyone earn decent wages. Decent wages went to white, married males. Women and minorities were paid less. Another downside was that the system was overly bureaucratic. It did not adjust well to change. As American industry came under fierce competition from abroad during the late 1960s, management experts "began to scapegoat the very business practices once considered to be the engine of growth, identifying them as accelerating America's decline." Social scientists devised new forms of work under the umbrella of "flexible specialization." In scholarship of the time, "A core expectation was that flexible work systems could be devised that not only would draw on workers' knowledge and judgment, but would privilege their knowledge above that of supervisors and managers . . . this innovation would create a basis for increasing the commitments of workers and lead to the convergence of their organizational interests with those of management" (Smith 1997).

Transforming the Workforce

The innovations have brought about new regimes, or approaches, to structuring work and organizing workers. The new regimes have left few workers untouched. An example of the new regimes is "job expansion." Job expansion means that workers learn and take on varied and multiple skills and tasks. That process enriches work lives. It also grants companies flexibility in staffing, which was not possible with the rigidly delineated skills and tasks of the industrial workplace. Another example is the creation of teams and work groups—manager-less, often temporary, bands of workers who are given responsibility for production and service in a particular area. The new regimes also have transformed company workforces. Instead of employing large cadres of permanent workers, businesses now engage numerous part-time and temporary people. These contingent workers allow companies to adjust easily and quickly to economic and production changes. (The bulk of temporary and part-time workers, who are paid less and are the first to be let go, are women and minorities.) Even so, the new approaches to doing work—such as job expansion and work teams—can in fact healthfully involve people in useful, concrete ways with their work and provide workers with promising new prospects.

Something Goes Amiss

Having tried to end workplace drudgery, social scientists are now raising troubling questions about the new work regimes. First, social scientists question whether these work changes—particularly in the light of downsizing companies have engaged in as they make these changes—are actually succeeding. Second, they question whether these changes are not themselves causing new kinds of psychological and emotional stress for workers. These questions are contentious. The research has come up with contradictory findings. But a notion doggedly persists that all is not right in the American workplace today. This notion is found not only in the work of a goodly number of sociologists, but it is also the belief of many workers.

Academic critics say that instead of empowering workers to make decisions, the new forms of work can instead impose new and impersonal means of control. This "decentered" authority, as social scientists call it, puts the responsibility for maintaining and increasing production squarely on workers and absolves managers of failure. Also, scholarly critics say work teams foster superficiality because the teams turn over regularly. Additionally, the once steady careers of middle-class, middle-level managers are decidedly less secure. Flattened bureaucracies and downsizings have hurt managers. Instead of getting promotions, as they once expected for good work, managers are being told to switch to different jobs in the company. Finally, workdays are growing in length and intensity. Taken together, the new regimes are leading to high levels of stress, frequent overwork, and job insecurity. But unlike in the old industrial economy, the average worker is not compensated with decent wages.

Eroded Values

Richard Sennett, a sociologist at New York University, is a prominent critic of the new work regimes. His perceptive essay, *The Corrosion of Character*, laments how companies expect work to be done today. Sennett says that work has historically been the source of personal identity. Work is the basis on which the core narratives of life that give meaning to individuals are built. The new regimes, as practiced in many companies, threaten those narratives. Sennett recalls a chance meeting of a man who was the son of a laborer Sennett had interviewed for a study many years before. Rico is among the new professionals with advanced degrees; his father, Enrico, had been a janitor with little education. Working hard, saving regularly, and playing by the rules, Enrico and his wife were able to buy a suburban house and send Rico to college. Both Rico and his wife, Jeannette, are part of the new economy, immersed in the new regimes of work. He is an independent technology consultant; she manages accountants scattered across the country.

Yet Rico is unhappy. He frets about his children. He worries that the values of the new workplace are not the values of the home. The new workplace erodes trust, loyalty, and mutual commitment. "You can't imagine how stupid I feel when I talk to my kids about commitment," Rico tells Sennett on the long evening flight to Europe where they bumped into each other. "It's an abstract virtue to them; they don't see it anywhere" (Sennett 1998). The new regimes have benefited people, freeing them from oppressive and overly stratified workplaces whose routines and dictates had to be endured day by day. But, as Sennett says, the new work regimes are also stripping people of constancy, sincerity, and steadfastness, the values on which good lives are built.

The Reshaping of Cities and Social Networks

During the height of industrialism in the 1950s and 1960s, years of loyal labor, regular savings, job advancement, automobile ownership, and newly earned college degrees (paid for by the GI Bill, a special benefit to war veterans) did bring many American families, like Enrico's, into the burgeoning suburbs for the first time. Urban blight took hold of the nation's central cities as families deserted the crowded old neighborhoods for tract homes with lawns outside the city. Postindustrialism has reversed parts of this trend. Some inner cities are thriving. In place of the urban ghettos that replaced the old neighborhoods, the suburbs into which people moved decades ago are now becoming mixed ethnically and economically.

From Rings to Nodules

The sources of our present understanding of the urban geography—indeed, much of what is known about cities—comes from a pair of urban sociologists at the University of Chicago in the early twentieth century. Ernest Burgess and Robert E. Park are the founders of the Chicago School of Urbanism. Burgess, Park, and other scholars depicted the typical city of the industrial period like this: around a central urban core of businesses and industries (that provided the jobs) and low-income neighborhoods (that were often ethnic) were rings of residential suburbs, each rising in affluence, as they moved ever outward toward rural precincts. Unfortunately, this depiction was not entirely accurate. Later scholars found that residents of the old inner residential rings of many U.S. cities were actually better off financially than residents of the outer rings. Industry and business were sometimes located in the suburbs, too (Harris and Lewis 1998). However, in the 1950s and 1960s, when the great migration to the suburbs took place in America, this Chicago school's depiction of cities—whether accurate or not before—turned into reality as jobs and people deserted the city. The suburbs became wealthier; inner cities became impoverished.

Then, in the 1970s, Thomas M. Stanback, an urban economist, and his colleagues saw a new pattern taking hold in American cities. "Outer cities" were emerging in the suburbs. Young professionals were returning to old urban neighborhoods. Stanback attributed this reshaping of the city to the growth of business and financial services (Noyelle and Stanback 1984). Companies were moving to where they could maximize their potential labor force: corporate headquarters and back offices to the suburbs; professional services to the city. Over the next two decades, American central cities were reborn with growing populations of professionals and bustling new office towers. Concentrated job centers—"nodules"—that varied from clusters of corporate offices to warehousing districts arose in the surrounding suburbs.[7] Poverty that had been confined to urban tenements began to appear in the suburbs, as did ethnic enclaves that were once exclusive to the inner cities.

Sassen says that the growth of "producer" services has reshaped the urban cores of many larger cities. The assortment of accounting, legal, marketing, consulting, and other firms to which corporations turn today are now settled in the midst of larger cities (Sassen 2001). These firms need to be in a place where they can find pools of talent and technological support and expertise. That place has turned out to be inside cities where cosmopolitan young professionals prefer to live. As a result of the growth of producer services, high-rise condominiums and apartments are being built in many cities, and old warehouses and factories are being converted into lofts and other residences. Take the city of Atlanta as an example. Over a few short years in the late 1990s and early 2000s, the city's downtown and midtown exploded with dozens of new high- and mid-rise apartments and condos. The city issued three times as many permits for multifamily units in 2001 as it did three years earlier, according to CENSTATS data. Chicago, too, is a preeminent example of the postindustrial transformation reshaping the central city. Thirty years ago, shorn of its manufacturing districts and most of its corporate headquarters, central Chicago lost many of its residents. Filled with the desperately poor, gang- and drug-ridden housing projects such as Cabrini Green and Henry Horner came to symbolize the city. But now the policy of replacing public housing with smaller and mixed projects has led the city's housing authority to demolish those infamous projects.

Where once stood part of Cabrini Green now stands a gleaming new Crate and Barrel outlet. Around the Chicago Loop, too, are spiffy new residential high-rises and housing conversions. Outside Chicago, suburbs are now made up of myriad nodules of employment, typical of which is Naperville, Illinois. Some of these nodules are large shopping and entertainment complexes that have come to symbolize the new urban geography.[8]

Choosing Where to Live

Residential places are growing both within and outside of cities. Instead of cities being dominated by impoverished ethnic communities and suburbs being characterized by affluent white families, cities are becoming more typified by the presence of young singles. Metropolitan areas are still characterized by demographically segregated residential places, but the nature of those locales is not like the forcibly segregated neighborhoods of industrial cities. The neighborhoods of industrial cities were usually segregated by religion, class, and ethnicity, as well as by proximity to jobs. Religion is not a factor in postindustrial residential places, but life cycle and income are factors, though these factors are difficult to measure (Fischer and Hout 2003). Though longstanding social prejudice and housing discrimination continues to play a role, the character of residential places is now more shaped by the affordability of housing, the caliber of public schools, the quality of community amenities, and the location of jobs. People make choices about where to live based on these factors. Of particular note is how suburban residential places have become more ethnic. Between 1990 and 2000, for example, the percentage of nonwhite suburban residents went from 33 to 40 percent around Atlanta, according to Census Bureau data. (The percentage of nonwhite residents in the city of Atlanta fell slightly.) An example of this racial and ethnic reformation of metropolitan areas is Washington, D.C. During the 1990s, many white professionals moved into the city, particularly on the district's west side, and African Americans relocated to suburban Prince George's County, Maryland. Large immigrant enclaves sprang up near Silver Spring, Maryland, and Arlington, Virginia.

Unbound Personal Ties

The changes in residential places have occurred in conjunction with changes in the location of social contacts. In the industrial city, neighborhoods were typically characterized by intense and multiple ties among residents. Neighbors were friends and colleagues. They met regularly in civic groups, churches, workplaces, recreational pursuits, school events, and so forth. Personal networks are no longer constrained by neighborhood geography. Personal networks extend around the city, if not the whole country and world. The personal networks of people do not overlap—have multiple ties with same people—as much as they once did (Fischer 1982). Sociologist Nancy L. Eiesland provides a good example of social networks in her portrait of two couples in Dacula, an emerging Atlanta exurb. The first couple, Vernon and Marie England, grew up in Dacula when it was a rural community. Nearly all of their family, friends, and contacts live there. They rarely venture beyond the town, especially for everyday needs. The second couple, Todd and Faith Pender, are newcomers. Few of their social contacts are in Dacula. No family member lives nearby. Todd works in an office park 20 miles away and plays softball on a team seven miles away. Before she quit work, Faith took the children to a day care eight miles from home. She then reversed direction to drive to her office in central Atlanta. Todd and Faith shop in malls. They visit friends scattered around Atlanta. In the new residential places, Eiesland says, "Families and individuals . . . make their own decisions about where to live, where to work, where to go to school, where to go shopping, and where (and if) to worship within the expanding matrix of particular places that make up the metropolitan region" (Eiesland 2000).

The postindustrial transformation has reshaped cities. A positive result of that reshaping is that people have greater choice about where to live and with whom to associate. But a negative result is a nagging sense that the community and constancy formerly found in places have been lost.

Changes in Mobility, Youth, and Old Age

Occurring in conjunction with the postindustrial transformation are three other important developments. These developments are the persistence of geographic mobility, the prolonged period of young adulthood, and the continued lengthening of life expectancy.

The Persistence of Geographic Mobility

The U.S. Census Bureau surveys say the percentage of Americans changing addresses each year dropped from about one in five to about one in six from the 1950s to the late 1990s. This decline is due to the fact that Americans are aging. Older people move less. Though annual rates of mobility have dropped, however, the actual number of moves people make during their lifetimes is likely unchanged, if it has not grown. People are living longer. They have more opportunities to move over a longer lifetime. Among younger people, mobility rates are extraordinary. At least a fourth of younger workers move every year. The percentage of movers among people under age 35 in professional occupations is more than triple that of similar jobholders age 35 and older. The moving rate among younger people in clerical and other administrative jobs is more than four times what is for older people in those occupations.[9] During the 1990s, the proportion of Americans who moved long distances rose. Also, mobility rates are now about the same regardless of household income and are no longer higher among the better educated.

Geographic mobility can create social and personal problems (Schachter 2001a; Schachter 2002b). Mobility weakens physical community and family networks (Fischer 1982). It generates psychological and emotional stress that is more common among poorer, less educated people, as sociologist Leo Strole found in the 1950s. Educated, urbane, and wealthier people adjust more easily and thus escape much of the associated psychological and emotional stress (Portes and Rumbaut 1996).

The Prolonging of Young Adulthood

The postindustrial economy demands education. As a result, the social maturity of the young is being postponed. In industrial society, many youth went to work after high school, if not before. Within a few years, they had wed and begun to raise children. In postindustrial society, the young are spending more years in school before taking a permanent job. They marry and have children at a later age. In 2000, the median ages at which men and women first married were about 27 and 25, respectively. In 1970, the median age of first marriage was about 23 and 21, respectively, based on Census Bureau data. The average age at which women bear their first child has risen 3.5 years since 1970, according to National Center for Health Statistics data. A slightly larger proportion of women than before are not marrying at all (Norton and Miller 1992) or having children ever (Bachu and O'Connell 2001).

As marriage and children are being postponed, the cheap and rich diet that is common to many economically advanced nations is causing the physical maturing of children at an earlier age. The number of obese children is rising, according to National Center for Health Statistics. An apparent effect of obesity is that girls develop sooner (Anderson, Dallal, and Must 2003; Davison, Susman, and Birch 2003), though sexual development is stalled among boys (Wang 2002). Consequently, the gap is widening between the age when young females, at least, are physically mature and when as adults they are socially mature, that is, assuming the burdens of work, marriage, and child-raising. This prolonged phase is exposing the young for a longer time to the ephemeral trends of youth cultures, feelings of social estrangement, and cravings for personal identity. As a group of scholars studying the extended time spent in young adulthood recently reported, "many young people have not become fully adult because they are not ready or able to perform the full range of adult roles, and they have not forged a stable identity of who they are and where they fit into society" (Furstenberg et al. 2004).

The Lengthening of Life Expectancy

Social maturity is being delayed for the young, but old age is being postponed for the elderly. Life expectancy is rising. In 2001, the life expectancy at birth for the average American was 77 years, according to National Center for Health Statistics estimates. Twenty years before, life expectancy was about 71 years. No end to rising life expectancy appears to be in sight. Scholars have even become uncertain how long humans can live. Some medical and biological scholars predict life spans of around 120 years (Himes 2001). According to one study, if present trends continue, life expectancy for women should reach about 100 years of age in the United States after mid-century (Vaupel and Oeppen 2002).

Lengthening longevity is increasing the *number* of older people. In the 2000 Census, about 35 million Americans were age 65 and over. About 4.2 million of them were age 85 and over. The size of the latter group has nearly tripled since 1970. Also, the *proportion* of the nation's residents who are older is increasing. One in every eight Americans was age 65 and over in the 2000 Census (Hetzel and Smith 2001). According to interim Census Bureau projections issued in 2003, the actual number of older adults is expected to more than double by 2030. Notably, the older generation today is the wealthiest, best educated, and perhaps healthiest that the nation has ever had (Treas 1995). Because people are staying agile longer, the proportion of older workers began to rise in the mid-1990s after falling for three decades, according to Census Bureau data.

A New Role for Religion and Congregations

Within a matter of decades, fundamental changes have taken place in social class, the workplace, and in the nature of communities and personal ties. These changes have affected religion and religious communities. But religion has not lost value in society or for individuals. Nor have religion or religious bodies become casualties of rising individualism, fading tradition, and shriveling rationality. What has happened is that religion and religious congregations have slipped their deeply placed anchors in social class and physical communities. These two developments have important implications on the social status of religious bodies and on the location of their members.

Religion and Class

The religious alignments of the old industrial classes were well established. Over a century ago, Max Weber, in *The Protestant Ethnic and the Spirit of Capitalism,* tied the evolution of the middle class and its religious values to the emergence of the modern economy (Weber 2002). Weber also declared that the middle class gave "religion the primary function of legitimizing their own life pattern and situation in the world" (Weber 1993). The downtrodden took to religions that offered salvation, while the middle class sought to justify its social position through religion. Karl Marx also linked class and religion. Alienated workers turned to religion in order to relieve their suffering, and religion was a means of social domination over workers (Christiano, Swatos, and Kivisto 2002).

Protestant theologian H. Richard Niebuhr recorded the link—albeit disparaging—between social class and specific Protestant denominations in his semisociological *The Social Sources of Denominationalism,* written in 1929. The middle class graced the pews of proper churches; the disinherited crowded the benches of energetic sects. Niebuhr writes: "The evil of denominationalism lies in the conditions which makes the rise of sects desirable and necessary: in the failure of the churches to transcend the social conditions which fashion them into caste-organizations . . ." (Niebuhr 1987).

Survey results found that the class basis for mainline Protestant denominations persisted over a half century after Niebuhr's classic book was published on religious caste. About 72 percent of Episcopalians said they were upper-middle class, but only 27 percent of Church of God members claimed that distinction (Roof and McKinney 1989). A recent study of GenXer religion deduced that, among other factors, the young still make choices about what to believe and to which congregation to belong based on class factors (Flory and Miller 2000).

Realigning Religion and Class

In postindustrial society, the alignment of religion with class is no longer the same, though the old ties between education and religious belief still persist in modified form. One way to measure the relationship of religion to social position is through the amount of education possessed by believers. Table 2.1, on page 42, shows the 1984–1985 and 2002 results of the General Social Survey, a random sample regularly conducted by the National Opinion Research Center at the University of Chicago. The survey divides people by their present religious preference into three shades of religious belief—liberal, moderate, and fundamentalist. As the table shows, in comparison with fundamentalists and moderates, a much higher proportion of people in religiously liberal bodies went to college (13 to 16 years of schooling), and a larger proportion of those people had advanced educations (17-plus years of schooling). The proportion of people with liberal affiliations who are highly educated is about 18 percent. The data show that the bulk of people identifying with religiously conservative bodies—identified as fundamentalist in the survey—have become better educated over the intervening two decades. Many of the adherents of religiously conservative bodies now hold high school diplomas and have received postsecondary schooling. Even so, the largest proportion of the highly educated (45 percent) identify themselves with theological liberal communities, while the least educated still gravitate toward communities that are religiously conservative (44 percent).

The degree of the change in the social position of religious believers, however, is more evident in a second set of GSS data. These surveys show that more people identifying with religiously conservative bodies say they have better jobs than their fathers did, and the proportion who say that has risen over the past decade. Table 2.2, on page 43, shows GSS data for 1987 and 2000. In the 2000 survey, about half of fundamentalists said they held a job whose status was higher than their father's job, about the same percentage as in 1987.[10] However, more than a quarter of the religiously liberal said in 2000 that they held a job whose status was lower than their father's, compared with about a fifth who in 1987 said they had a lower status job. Status slippage is also apparent for people identified with religiously moderate faiths. These figures, combined with the education data, indicate that in recent decades, the religiously conservative have gained in status. But the religiously liberal and moderate are still perched at the top educationally.

In industrial society, the middle class was entrenched in liberal and moderate faiths, and the laboring class was positioned in conservative ones. Yet, as the previous data indicates, new professionals appear to gravitate toward liberal faiths, which are found in mainline bodies, and the service and technical occupational class is more attracted to conservative beliefs, though moderate beliefs are also present. Vestiges of class-based

The Postindustrial Promise

Table 2.1: Number of Years of Education by Religious Orientation, 1984-1985 and 2002

Religious Orientation	Years of Education							
	8 Years or less		9 to 12 Years		13 to 16 Years		17 Years or more	
	1984-1985	2002	1984-1985	2002	1984-1985	2002	1984-1985	2002
Liberal	7.0%	2.6%	40.3%	37.2%	39.4%	42.5%	13.3%	17.7%
Moderate	10.1%	5.7%	51.2%	39.7%	30.4%	43.2%	8.4%	11.4%
Fundamentalist	15.5%	7.8%	57.1%	46.0%	23.2%	39.5%	4.3%	6.8%
(Number of Respondents)	(324)	(135)	(1,471)	(1,091)	(887)	(1,053)	(243)	(300)

SOURCE: General Social Survey, 1984-1985 and 2002.

Table 2.2: How Offspring Compared Their Job Status with Father's, 1987 and 2000

Religious Affiliation of Respondent:	Compared to Respondent, Father had:					
	Lower Job Status		About Equal Job Status		Higher Job Status	
	Survey Year		Survey Year		Survey Year	
	1987	2000	1987	2000	1987	2000
Liberal Congregation	21.2%	26.2%	28.7%	27.4%	43.2%	41.1%
Moderate Congregation	24.5%	27.8%	22.4%	22.0%	48.0%	45.0%
Fundamentalist Congregation	18.4%	19.0%	18.8%	24.5%	50.5%	51.4%
(Number of Respondents)	(307)	(259)	(324)	(260)	(693)	(484)

Not shown are data for respondents with no job, no father, or had a father with no job.
SOURCE: General Social Survey, 1987 and 2000.

religion still persist within the occupational classes. But these ties between religion and occupation class are not as direct as before with social class. Some well-educated people are strongly conservative; some
marginally educated are religiously liberal. The reason for the changed
ties is that religious leanings found in the occupational classes are derived from passed down religious narratives of the people within those
occupational classes. Those leanings are reinforced and reworked to fit
the social and religious situations that surround people. In a study of
American and French working men, Michèle Lamont, a Harvard University sociologist, found a sense of class identity persisting through the
moral views of workers. These moral views arose both from the workers' social backgrounds and from the conditions of their present life
(Lamont 2000).[11]

The New Religious Leanings

How economic and social situations affect religious leanings is not as
clear in postindustrial society as it was in industrial society. In his pio-
neering analysis of religion and class, Max Weber split classes into the
privileged and disprivileged (Weber 1993). The economic and educational status of the service and technical class is light-years from the
laboring class of Weber's day. It is hard to imagine them as disprivileged.
In fact, the most dramatic and visible religious changes of our time have
occurred among the service and technical occupational class. These
changes include the rapid growth of evangelicalism and the emergence
of new congregational styles. Drawn largely from the ranks of the old
blue-collar class and lower middle class, this occupational group is tied
to the religious narratives of conservative and moderate faiths. In the
postindustrial transformation, this class has advanced in education and
status and taken on jobs that are freed of the regimentation of the old
industrial order. On the other hand, this class is being touched more
negatively by the growth of two-earner families, the fluidity of residential communities, the dispersion of personal networks, and the preva-
lence of geographic mobility. For people in this occupational class, older
religious narratives have been reworked in order to steady their lives
morally and to provide a needed sense of self-worth.

Among the new professionals, religious change has also occurred.
But the religious changes that have transpired among this class are not
as profound as and are unlike the changes among the service and technical class. Because of their greater education, the new professionals are
more able to navigate the changes in relationships, communities, and

mobility than the service and technical class. But at the same time, demographic change has buffered the new professionals. More evident among this class is prolonged young adulthood, delays in marriage and childbirth, and the increase in life expectancy. Also, the new professionals are troubled by a degree of financial and occupational insecurity that did not exist in the old middle class.

Not to be forgotten are the working poor and the desperately poor. These occupational classes, who possess conservative religious narratives, are plagued by dropping wages, declining prospects, and weakening social ties. They represent what Weber called the salvation-seeking disprivileged. But the desperately poor are missing from religious bodies. Scholars have noted that many congregations, including ethnic ones located in places with many poor, have few members that are part of the underclass (Smith 2001; Laudarji and Livezey 2000; and McRoberts 2003).

Congregations and Place

Among congregations, the most evident change of the postindustrial transformation is that local religious bodies are no longer tied to physical communities in the way they were in the past. Congregations have been pulled from their geographic anchorages. Many congregations derive their memberships from social networks spread over wide geographic areas. The exceptions are geographically fixed congregations. These are congregations with assigned ecclesiastical boundaries, as in the Roman Catholic Church, or congregations that have decided to be bound to a particular neighborhood and the people who live within it (Livezey 2000).

Geographic location still has relevancy for congregations, however. As we have seen, social networks are homogeneous. Because residential places are still segregated by age and income, social networks tend to lodge in particular residential places and not others. Even so, the congregation may not be near the residential places in which the social networks within the congregation are clustered. Of course, parishes, real or assumed, are still tied to a specific geography, but even the congregations within those parishes may be divided intentionally, or unintentionally, into various subgroups by ethnicity, age, and other social and demographic factors. Moreover, some religious bodies—such as megachurches—have moved to sites that are meant to be independent of physical communities. The congregations have settled in these places because the sites are near highway junctions or because the sites are affordable.

Examples of congregations and the changed connection to geography abound in congregations visited as part of The Church in Postindustrial America project.

- Central Baptist Church, a socially activist body in Wayne, a well-to-do Philadelphia suburb, draws most of its members from around the city, as well as neighboring Delaware and New Jersey. But virtually none of its members come from Wayne, though that church has sat on the main street of the town for over a century.

- Another Baptist church, Tenth Memorial, located in poverty stricken north Philadelphia, draws its members from its community and from around the metropolitan area. A block away from Tenth Memorial's building, a roving police patrol regularly occupies a street corner in order to deter drug dealers. Leading the African American church is a politically connected pastor, Dr. William B. Moore. Tenth Memorial erected a high-rise for the elderly and sponsored new family housing within blocks of its building and is engaged in ministries to bolster families and to help inner-city youth.

- Templo Calvario, a large Hispanic Pentecostal church, is housed in a warehouse in Santa Ana, California, that provides a cost-effective space to do ministry. That ministry includes a massive collection and distribution effort that utilizes a giant cooler still in the warehouse to support food pantries at other churches. Some of Templo Calvario's worshipers live nearby but most now come from throughout Orange County, which has a growing Hispanic presence.

- A Roman Catholic parish, St. Mark's in Dorchester, Massachusetts, concentrates on community organizing within its square-mile territory. The once solidly Irish parish is losing Catholics, the exception being new Vietnamese and Caribbean families. St. Mark's sponsors neighborhood watches, housing renovation, economic development, community beautification, and leadership training.

Amid the myriad changes in class, work, and geography that have disordered society, the ties of religious bodies to social position and physical communities have also changed. More importantly, religious congregations have become places in which people build bonds, work through troubles, and as the next chapter explores, reestablish their religious and cultural narratives.

Chapter 3

The Right Place for Me

"All of us are immigrants spiritually," wrote Walter Lippman a century ago. "We are all of us immigrants in the industrial world, and we have no authority to lean upon. We are an uprooted people, newly arrived, and nouveau riche."

Immigrants from eastern and southern Europe were landing at American ports in great numbers in the early twentieth century. The child of immigrants who had become a prominent columnist and social critic, Lippman was describing the disordered conditions of America's industrial age, both for the immigrant and for citizens whose ancestral ties to the nation ran deeply (Lippman 1990). Though Lippman was not much interested in their religion, the immigrants of this time were flooding into Catholic and Orthodox parishes, packing synagogues, and founding even more national variants of Lutheran, Reformed, and Baptist churches.

In a new wave of immigration that began in the late 1960s, people are again arriving in great numbers at U.S. borders and airports, but this time in a disordered postindustrial world. Today, as in Lippman's time, newly founded immigrant religious bodies—a number of them now Buddhist, Hindu, and Muslim—are having an enormous impact on the nation's religiosity and have made the United States the most religiously diverse country in the world (Eck 2001).

But the implications on religious bodies of this wave of new people and new religions goes beyond how the ethnic and religious composition of the population is changing. Another important implication is how immigration is reconfiguring the cultural substance of religious bodies. A recent surge of academic interest in the newest immigrants has uncovered a movement toward cultural retention. This new research has in fact identified a development in immigrant congregations that illustrates how the postindustrial transformation has reconfigured U.S. congregations. This chapter contends that this reconfiguration among American congregations—immigrant and otherwise—shows up in three basic trends. First, faith communities are now important places in which people establish or reestablish a particular cultural narrative. Second, congregations have responded to changes more or less intuitively, and that response has often been socially and religiously appropriate. Third, the trend among American congregations is toward many divergent forms and styles built around many religious and demographic contexts. This chapter also looks at sociological developments in understanding society and the position of religion in society that pertain to these developments in congregations. By looking at studies of congregations in Dacula, Georgia, and Naperville, Illinois, this chapter also explores how diversity in congregational form and style helps faith bodies not only adapt successfully to change but also serve people socially and religiously.

Changes in Immigrant Congregations

During the previous wave of massive immigration, before being cut short by a nativist backlash in the 1920s, immigrants who came to America arrived in an industrial nation. Largely unskilled and rural, these immigrants lived in the crowded tenements of the growing manufacturing metropolises of the northeastern and midwestern United States. Life was rough and tough, but before these immigrants, and especially their children, lay the prospect of becoming American, a process in which religion had a role. As Will Herberg, a noted observer of American religion in the 1950s, said:

> Sooner or later the immigrant will give up virtually everything he had brought with him from the "old country"—his language, his nationality, his manner of life—and will adopt the ways of his new home. Within broad limits, however, his becoming an American did not involve his abandoning the old religion in favor of some native American substitute. Quite the contrary, not only was he expected to retain his old religion, as he was not expected to retain his old language or nationality, but such was the shape of America that it was largely in and through his religion that he, or rather his children and grandchildren, found an identifiable place in American life. (Herberg 1983)

In this past wave of immigration, religious communities helped immigrants to assimilate into a common American culture. For example, after initially fostering the establishment of "national" parishes catering to a particular ethnicity, the Roman Catholic bishops in the United States turned to "Americanizing" parishes and parishioners. The starting of new nonethnic organizations in parishes and the early use of English in the business of the parish were among attempts to speed assimilation (Shaw 1998).

From Melting Pot to Bouillabaisse

But the wholesale assimilation of the past has been replaced today by what social scientists call "segmented" assimilation (Portes and Rumbaut 1996). In segmented assimilation, immigrants adopt parts of American culture but resist other parts. Present-day immigrants do not give up their manner of life as readily as Herberg said they did many decades ago. Ethnic cultures are more resilient today, and they are likely to stay resilient.[1] The classic and somewhat erroneous picture of the United States was of a melting pot in which all the elements were eventually reduced to a uniform texture.[2] This image is strikingly inaccurate in the present time when, once again, numerous Americans declare themselves of foreign birth[3] because this time immigrant cultures have staying power. Today, instead of depicting the United States as a melting pot, the country is better seen as a spicy and chunky bouillabaisse.

These changes in assimilation are related to changes in the immigrants themselves. Besides the fact that the bulk of immigrants are now from Latin America and Asia, and are more racially and ethnically diverse than before, the main differences between present immigrants and those in the past are in education and skills. Not all of the immigrants who arrive in America now are "your tired, your poor, your huddled masses," as the poem by Emma Lazarus says on the base of the Statue of Liberty. Instead, many immigrants teach in the nation's universities, research in its laboratories, and care for the ill in its hospitals and clinics. They are entrepreneurs who start corporations or run the corner store. Yet, other immigrants are not so educationally and occupationally advantaged. Some cut grass, scrub hotel rooms, and hammer nails. They hustle in meatpacking plants and toil in illegal sweatshops. The reason for this stark split among immigrants is that the postindustrial economy demands both high-wage professionals and low-wage laborers (see chapter 2). The result is that immigrants flowing into the United States come in two streams: the highly skilled and the less skilled. Unfortunately for the less skilled, the middle rungs of the ladder of opportunity that enabled the children of immigrants to progress economically and socially

are missing. Particularly for immigrants trapped in impoverished enclaves with bad schools, the postindustrial need for education has opened
a yawning gap over which the children of immigrants cannot easily step.
"A college education, previously a dream accomplished after three or
four generations in America, must now be acquired in the course of one,"
say immigration scholars Alejandro Portes and Ruben G. Rumbaut
(Portes and Rumbaut 1996).

Protecting the Children

These problems with postindustrial society are a reason for the shift more
toward cultural retention and away from cultural assimilation. Of course,
immigrants today find it easier to retain tight ties with their homelands,
and thus their culture, in ways that were not possible a century ago. You
can call your mother weekly, or e-mail your brother nightly. You can fly
home to your sister's wedding and be back in days. Immigrants see
cultural retention as the means to help their children succeed educationally and occupationally. Studies of new immigrants have found that
many immigrant parents fear the influence of American popular culture on their children (Warner and Wittner 1998; Yang 1999; Ebaugh and
Chafetz 2000). These immigrant parents believe that popular culture—
which through its music, movies, and other media devalues education,
achievement, and family life and plays up sex, drugs, and gangs—erodes
the personal hardiness and moral persistence children need to get a good
degree and land a decent job. (The desire to protect children from gangs,
drugs, and crime can be so strong that scholars have found instances of
parents sending children *back* to their homelands for school.) Unless
cultural assimilation is resisted, immigrants believe their children will
waste away in pitiable careers (in the case of immigrant professionals)
or toil in jobs as lowly as their own (in the case of immigrant laborers).
Either outcome is bitter: having come to America, they will have failed
to make a better life for their children.

  These fears have led many immigrants to religious bodies. As sociologist Warner says, immigrant parents have noticed that "religion is
their key to cultural reproduction" (Warner and Wittner 1998).[4] Congregations are places where culture can be reembodied, as religious scholar
Dorothy C. Bass contends. Bass says the genius of congregations is "in
their ability to express the particularity of a people" and "link people to
something that extends over the centuries and across the nations" (Bass
1998).[5] Academic research has found many cases where congregations
are helping people to retain at least part of their ethnic culture because

that culture supplies the resilience needed in postindustrial society. The exception is in some Pentecostal and evangelical congregations where religious culture has replaced ethnic culture or the congregations downplay ethnic culture.

In most cases among Protestant and Catholic bodies, however, congregations intertwine religious and ethnic cultural narratives. As Fenggang Yang, a sociologist of religion at Purdue University, says of the rapid growth of evangelical Christianity among Chinese immigrants in the United States, "evangelical Christianity provides the needed certainty and absoluteness. The evangelical ethnic church also helps these Chinese immigrants to selectively preserve traditional moral values that are perceived as compatible with Christian beliefs, and thus helps them to reconstruct their distinctive Chinese identity" (Yang 1998). Academic studies have noted other ways that congregations help immigrants. Religious bodies help solidify identities, supply emotional support, assist the needy, and assail social problems. Religious bodies have become popular among immigrants at a time when religion was supposedly losing steam in the United States. Some immigrants are known to switch religious faiths—even become religious—because the religious congregations of their coethnics are so supportive.

Acting on Their Own

In present-day immigrant congregations, the role that many religious bodies have taken in assimilation has *not* come about because of an edict from upon high, unlike in the last wave of immigration. Few national religious bodies today even view their efforts to plant and support immigrant congregations as a means to speed social and religious assimilation, as Protestant and Catholic groups did a century ago. Indeed, many immigrants are planting congregations that are independent of, or loosely affiliated with, any larger formal religious organization. Immigrant religious bodies are acting on their own. Warner identifies this trend among immigrant religious bodies, a movement toward localized congregational organization and decision making, as de facto congregationalism. He says the trend has occurred not only among immigrant Christian churches but also among Buddhist temples, Hindu shrines, and Muslim masjids, bodies in religious faiths that have never had congregational forms (Warner 1998a). Warner's work has been borne out in studies of immigrant bodies in Chicago and Houston (Ebaugh and Chafetz 2000; Livezey 2000). Notably, Warner also says that this movement toward de facto congregationalism is occurring among all American religious bodies—immigrant and otherwise—regardless of any particular institution's theology or structure. Local religious bodies are going their own way and becoming theologically, if not demographically, homogeneous bodies unconstrained by neighborhood geography (Warner 1998a). Congregants are shaping their own local religious bodies. The leadership, theology, or polity of a particular religious expression have become less influential within local bodies.

These findings from studies of immigrant congregations illustrate how the postindustrial transformation has reconfigured the role of congregations. Immigrant religious bodies are where people reembody cultural narratives. They are where people reroot themselves. This reconfiguration is not limited to immigrant bodies; it is analogous to what is happening among all American communities of faith.

Developments in Social Sciences

Helpful to understanding what has happened among congregations and religion are several developments in the social sciences. What is important about these developments to religious leaders and their communities is that these developments also provide new ways of thinking about congregations. The development of particular interest is newer concepts of a social system. As an idea, social systems have been around in sociology for some time. American sociologist Talcott Parsons pioneered the idea a half century ago. A number of difficulties have plagued his theory, however, and it has fallen to the wayside. Newer social system theory is alluring, however, because it explains present-day social changes more adequately than the older sociological theory discussed in chapter 1. Social systems theory offers insights into religion and the role of religion in society that are more helpful to explaining postindustrial society.

New Social System Theory

Social system theory drops two ideas inherent to modern and postmodern theory. Modern and postmodern theories were, of course, developed during the rise and at the height of industrial society, periods in which American society was more rigidly fixed by class, work, and religion. Modern and postmodern theories embrace ideas of rigid and stratified social structure. Modern and postmodern theory has also pointed to the loss of the cultural narratives with the collapse of the old industrial order, cultural narratives that the theories consider vital to society. These cultural narratives are stories that tell how life is to be lived and provide people with unity and purpose. These narratives on a personal level are "the instruction manuals in our imaginations" (Wuthnow 1993). In a larger form, these narratives are the protective "sacred canopy" that Berger said sheltered society and people from meaninglessness.

The problems created for sociology because of the collapse of the old structures and the unraveling of the big cultural narratives resulted because older social theory is so tied to its ideas about structure and narrative. In ditching those concepts of fixed structure and overarching narrative, social system theory avoids many of the problems that have recently plagued the social sciences. Social systems theory has structure, too, but in systems theory, that structure is flexible and not fixed. Moreover, the breaking up of overarching cultural narratives is not a problem for social systems because social systems function differently than fixed social structures and do not necessarily require intact, overarching narratives.

The primary author of new social systems theory is Niklas Luhmann, a German sociologist. This unusual and largely self-taught scholar, who until his death in 1998 was at the University of Bielefeld in Germany, formulated a complete new theory of society. His primary theory is summarized in his book published in 1984 as *Soziale Systeme*, and translated as *Social Systems* into English in 1995. Luhmann's theory is partly based on the work of earlier sociologists, including Talcott Parsons, as well as a few scientists in other fields.

Luhmann's theory is formidable. But three points in his theory are particularly relevant to understanding the nature of the postindustrial society. First, instead of seeing society as rigidly fixed, Luhmann says society consists of complex and evolving social systems and their subsystems. Second, these social systems and their subsystems are not manipulated from the top, as in industrial society, but instead are largely self-organizing, an ability that Luhmann calls "autopoiesis." Third, in his theory of society, meaning is not a social idea that is lost with the dilution of larger cultural narratives or the collapse of sacred canopies (as Peter Berger contended). Meaning is always present (Luhmann 1999).

Putting Religion on Solid Footing

The way that Luhmann's theory pertains to religion and to the place of religion in society is not fully clear among U.S. sociologists because not all of his work on religion has been translated into English and because of the fact that Luhmann's work is unusually abstract. Fortunately, a Canadian sociologist of religion, Peter Beyer, has filled in some of the gaps of how Luhmann's theory pertains to religion. Beyer also provides a basis for adapting Luhmann's abstractions to the particular circumstances of postindustrial society. Though Beyer, a lecturer at the University of Ottawa, focuses on the role of religion in a global context, his ideas can apply to a local context. Three points that Beyer makes are helpful to understanding how religion and religious bodies have changed in recent times. The first point is that religion functions in society by two means. First, religion has a role in all social subsystems. Second, religion has its own social subsystem. In one form, religion is a key means by which systems reorganize themselves and make choices when faced with new circumstances, and in the other form, religion as a system, it is a means to address moral dilemmas, such as the public issues of poverty, sexuality, oppression, abortion, and so forth. This idea of how religion is entrenched in society is compelling because it explains how religious ideas not only persist but are deeply held in the face of cultural pluralism and how religion can be a potent force in public discourse. In older social theory, religion didn't have a leg to stand on; in social system theory, religion has two solid legs on which to perch.

The Mainline Is No Longer the Norm

Beyer's second point is a revelation about the role of middle-class and mainline religion. A crucial difference exists between the place of religion in industrial society and its place in postindustrial society. In industrial society, the religious ideas that were held up as normal were usually those of the middle class and mainline religious groups. As Beyer says, society's top levels "usually attempted to style their religion as definitive for the society as a whole, often in the form of an overarching cosmology that made the norms and values of the upper strata, including their moral code, the presumptive standard for all behavior. . . . The overarching religious ideologies did not have to penetrate to the popular strata, only to claim relevance for these as well" (Beyer 1994). As such, the old middle class was able to push its particular religion on society as the proper standard. In this country, the middle class has never found it easy to impose its values, though it decidedly frowned on religious groups that did not conform to its norms. With the fading of social class, no class can now easily impose its religion over another. Mainline religion has ceased to be the norm. It has lost stature. But mainline religion has not lost relevance to its adherents. Mainline religion remains potent to its adherents, who, as was noted in the previous chapter, are now largely part of the professional class. What mainline religion can no longer do is claim relevance for everyone else, a relevance that mainline faiths never had in fact. Nor is the professional class in a position to declare its religion as the cultural norm. The professional class and its religion is heavily outnumbered by the service and technical class and that group's more popularly based mixture of moderate and evangelical faiths. Mainline religion is not being pushed aside for sudden want of relevancy. It is being pushed aside by the sheer weight of numbers, and it is numbers, not social position, that generally grant stature or power now.

Emerging Group Cultures

A third point that Beyer makes is about how Luhmann pictures the construction of society. Society is made up of systems, organizations, and interactions—the latter basically people encountering each other in some fashion. Contemporary society is less stratified, and as a result, encounters are freed from restraints organizations once imposed on them. Unrestrained encounters give rise to group cultures formed out of people who are similar in some way. These group cultures, which are subcultures, are made up of social networks and organizations. As Beyer says, "Group culture often manifests itself in the regular interactions of social networks." Organizations are positioned within group cultures. The role that an organization plays within a group culture is as an institution that helps define and maintain that group culture and its identity. The institution does not control the group culture, however. This description of organizations and cultures resembles scholarly portrayals of the relationship of immigrant religious bodies to ethnic cultures. Immigrant religious bodies are instrumental to sustaining the vitality of the ethnic culture.

Congregations and Community Change

Contributing to our understanding of social systems and religion is a study by Nancy Eiesland of a fast-growing Sunbelt exurb, though her work is not strictly about social systems. This sociologist spent several years studying churches in Dacula, Georgia. What Eiesland focuses on is organizational ecology, that is, how local religious bodies operate within a local context with respect to each other and to individuals, which is similar to systems theory. Eiesland settled on an ecological approach after finding that rational choice theory, with its stress on competing religious groups, was not a good fit with what was going on in Dacula. Eiesland says, "The religious ecology is not a ceaseless round of skirmishes of groups, organizations, and individuals, caught in a win-lose area of combat and death" (Eiesland 2000).

Eiesland found in Dacula that congregations adapted to community change mainly through the social networks of their members, that the adaptation to community change led to greater diversity in local religious bodies, and that congregations were—in some sense—self-adapting to change. Eiesland says that the extent of church members' personal networks was related to the capability of local religious bodies to adapt to rapid change in Dacula. The more widespread members' networks, the greater chance the congregation had to adapt to change: "Local knowledge, culture, and networks give shape to organizations that have greater flexibility; and within ecologies this diversity enables adaptability among the population of organizations." In fact, congregations that held strict beliefs, and in which members had tight and closed networks, had sabotaged their ability to navigate Dacula's rapid change. Thus, one long-established church, Hinton Memorial, was able to adjust to change; however, another long-established church, Felding Chapel, died because it had no means to adjust. The way a congregation is positioned within social networks leads not to an acculturation that causes the church to shirk its religious mission. As Eiesland points out, "whatever other ends they [these congregations] may serve, their original and continuing identity is religious."

Diversity Is the Key to Adaption

Eiesland also says change made the local religious ecology more diverse. New churches showed up in town. Existing congregations were reshaped in different ways. The local Methodist church, once at the apex of religious life in old Dacula, lost stature to a rapidly growing Baptist body. Eiesland found that by becoming more diverse, rather than following the same course as each other, Dacula's congregations were able to successfully adapt to community change. Congregations become either generalist or specialist organizations. Generalist bodies appealed to a broad population and often had complex and large organizations with many subgroups, as was the case in Dacula for Hebron Baptist, the local megachurch. Specialist bodies appealed to underserved populations, were atypical organizationally, or addressed specialized community needs, as eventually did Hinton Memorial, now First United Methodist.

Notably, Luhmann's idea that social systems spawn increasing complexity is reflected in Dacula's growing diversity.

In Eiesland's book are found tinges of Luhmann's notion of autopoiesis. Congregations were able to respond to community change through their social networks without being directed by a central source, such as a pastor. Eiesland explains:

> By focusing on the linkages created by individuals within religious organizations, this study moves away from the emphasis on the entrepreneurial leader as the primary agent of adaptation. The interweaving of participants' routines of religious belonging can produce significant alteration in local congregations. When leadership fails or is unable to envision strategies of action that respond to alterations in their environment, congregants may respond by drawing on knowledge and resources devised from participation within other religious groups as well as other types of organizations. (Eiesland 2000)

Religious bodies are tied to social networks, and those networks form the basis of cultures in which congregations are positioned. As institutions, congregations help to define and maintain those cultures. Because of their linkages to social networks, congregations are able to adapt to change within their community. Adaptation can happen through the collective contacts and knowledge of congregants, rather than just through entrepreneurial leadership. As congregations respond to change, too, they are becoming more diverse because their responses are different.

Treading Divergent Paths

Paul D. Numrich, a sociologist at Chicago's Loyola University, has captured the anxiety that permeates an otherwise well-to-do suburb outside of Chicago in a study of its congregations. Populated by many members of the professional class, as well as some of the service and technical class, Naperville—without debate—offers a high standard of living. Naperville is also the quintessential postindustrial suburb. The home of corporate headquarters and research laboratories, the growing town is an employment nodule like those discussed in chapter 2. Located nearby, for example, are high-profile scientific endeavors: the Argonne National Laboratory and the Fermi National Accelerator Laboratory. Numrich says, "Naperville strikes many observers as the postindustrial metropolitan success story, having made the transition from quaint small town to thriving technoburb" (Numrich 2000).

But the dark side of the postindustrial transformation is also found there. Naperville is a transitory community, for example. Besides frequent job transfers, sudden layoffs brought on by economic changes and corporate restructuring are also too common to residents. Life in the DuPage County, Illinois, suburb has been the subject of magazine articles, as well as a book on working women. These accounts have noted the personal stress, vocational anxieties, and social problems that seem to haunt people in what seems like it should be an idyllic and leisurely town.[6]

Changing Lives and Changing Congregations

In Naperville, too, can be seen the effects of the postindustrial transformation on local religious bodies. As in Dacula, congregations in Naperville have been reconfigured in diverse ways as those bodies have adapted to changes in people's lives. This engagement with people takes place within a religious context, as Numrich describes in a local Lutheran church:

> Most of the congregation are middle-class professionals who suffer from vocational stress, overextension, and anxiety about downsizing. Saint James has responded by trying to create a comfortable, face-to-face community where harried, unappreciated, and anxious people can take heart that God loves them and calls them to a life of love in an often unloving society. People know each other here and share a friendly Christian fellowship together. (Numrich 2000)

St. James was one of about 60 Naperville communities of faith in existence at the time of Numrich's study. Those congregations range from nine churches historically tied to Naperville—mostly Baptist, Catholic, Congregational, and Methodist—to bodies that have sprung up more recently, including Saint James. Some of the newer congregations are evangelical and Pentecostal, as well as Jewish, Muslim, and Buddhist, and count among their members the town's newer Chinese, Korean, and Vietnamese residents. Some scholars have contended that new-paradigm congregations, large "seeker" sensitive bodies led by entrepreneurial pastors, are the religious standard of our time and will be the winners among American congregations (Sargeant 2000; Miller 1997).[7] New paradigm congregations are useful and valuable adaptations, but in Naperville, Numrich found, they appeared to be only one form of adaptation. Something other than that paradigm has taken hold in many congregations.

Five Naperville Congregations

Five of the Naperville congregations illustrate how religious bodies have the inherent ability to navigate postindustrial change. These five congregations are also good examples of the ways that congregations are vital and important places for people. The five are Saint James, Calvary Church, Wheatland Salem, First Church, and Beth Shalom, discussed below.[8]

- The 300-member Saint James is a theologically middle-of-the-road congregation made up mostly of middle-aged professionals. Founded in 1979, the church first met in a local school and later built a church near a busy major intersection. Unfortunately, the church site was too close to Fox Valley Mall on Highway 59, and a large store eventually hid the low silhouette of the church building. Unfortunately, too, the founding pastor quit after four years, an episode that cost the church members and deflated morale. Saint James is known as a small and intimate church and has advertised itself that way. Dress during worship at Saint James is casual, and the music is a mixture of contemporary and traditional. Not long after Numrich finished studying Naperville, Saint James put its site up for sale and bought land in neighboring Aurora. In the summer of 2003, the church left its building and again moved into a school for its worship services while it raised money for a new building. Despite its problems, Saint James is clearly a valuable place for its members. Numrich paraphrases the words of one member: "The church allows people to express their faith and to enrich their lives in ways not found on the job or in the neighborhood. One simply does not discuss certain things with one's neighbors. Also, since many members have no extended family in the area, the one continuity in their lives becomes church membership."

- More than a mile south from Saint James' old site on Highway 59 is Calvary Church. Unlike Saint James, Calvary is in a huge and easily visible building set on a large lot. The church dates to the late 1960s. Calvary is a Pentecostal megachurch that does not hide its faith: its cross looms over Highway 59. Sermons are long. People speak in tongues; arms are upraised toward God. An altar call concludes the service. It stresses moral conduct. More so than Saint James, Calvary is for people who have found the world a tough fit. Its ministry, which includes Christian counseling, support groups for the divorced, and events for single parents, focuses on troubled people. In addition to its well-attended worship services, Calvary has small fellowship groups where people discuss intimate and painful events in their lives and that are known to engage in lengthy, heartfelt prayer for recently fired coworkers, the ill, and the morally irresponsible. As an assistant pastor is quoted by Numrich, Calvary is not for everyone. "The key is whether a person's pain is great enough to risk anything to find healing, even walking into a Pentecostal church," says Numrich.

- East of Highway 59 on 95th Street is Wheatland Salem Church. In 1997, this Methodist church relocated from a small plot on the corner of Highway 59 and 95th Street to a 14-acre site amid tract homes. The congregation was formed from two Brethren churches German prairie farmers founded in the mid-nineteenth century. Despite its rural beginning, the evangelical congregation into which Wheatland Salem has evolved does not have the close personal ties found at Saint James. What brings 600 people—many of them young parents and children—to the church each week are "particular programs for themselves or their children, engaging worship experiences, and/ or the opportunity to participate in meaningful Christian volunteer opportunities," Numrich says. "These members certainly expect to be treated warmly and cordially in their relationships with other church folks, but they also seem to value a degree of distance and privacy." Wheatland Salem fits the lives of many people in Naperville. Savvy sermons deal with daily issues that confront members, as indicated by the title of the sermon one Sunday that Numrich visited: "When Maalox Moments Become a Way of Life."

- Unlike the old rural ties of Wheatland Salem, the roots of First Church are in town. Unlike Wheatland Salem, too, the original plans of this church, founded in 1833, to move—in this case off the heights overlooking Naperville's old commercial district to a suburban site— never came off. First Church stayed put in a historic limestone structure with stained-glass windows along the graceful tree-lined streets of Piety Hill, as the town's church district is nicknamed. Until the 1970s, the church had lost members as the township's center of population shifted to farmland south of Naperville proper. In the late 1990s, a planning committee recommended that the church move to a suburban site, turning the old building into a community center. First Church moved ahead to buy a new site, but the congregation had second thoughts. Instead of the church moving, a number of members left to form a church on the new site in 1998. Today, First Church has about 350 members, about twice the number of its suburban offspring, Hope Church. First Church sees its role as re-claiming the "disaffected." Besides having a strong sense of history, First Church is characterized by its liberal theology and commit-ment to social mission. The address for the church Web site does not carry the church name, but plays on the word *justice*. Not only does First Church identify itself as a "just peace" church, it is also an "open and affirming" body, the stamp for a church in its denomination that welcomes gays and lesbians.

• Not far from Piety Hill and Naperville's old-line churches is a newer congregation, Beth Shalom, a Reconstructionist synagogue. Though dating back to the 1970s, the synagogue did not build a facility until 1998. In a town that is nearly all Catholic and Protestant, Beth Sha-lom is emblematic of the growing diversity there among faith bod-ies. But Jews are still scarce in Naperville, and Beth Shalom is the only game in town for them, whether Progressive, Reformed, Con-servative, or Orthodox. With about 350 families, Beth Shalom prides itself on its *haimishness*. This intense emphasis on community ap-pears much in demand. Mobility is so frequent in Naperville that not one person in the synagogue has been there since the synagogue's beginning. Even on key religious holidays, many people still head to hometown synagogues to celebrate. But Beth Shalom helps people recapture their Judaism in a town overrun with Christians. Com-peting against people's hectic schedules (and Friday night high-school football in the fall), the synagogue strives through its programs to promote the basics of Jewish identity and reacquaint people with elements of their religion in a town, that, as one member says, has the feel of the Diaspora.

These five religious bodies—as well as other congregations in Naperville—have adapted in diverse ways to the needs of local people. Though adaptation has not always been easy, the congregations are fill-ing real and significant religious niches. By making these adaptations, these congregations have taken on diverse shapes that serve people in religiously and socially appropriate ways. Numrich points to the ability of Naperville's congregations to address the "stresses of edge-city life, offering religion's transcendent perspective, and spiritual comfort to people."[9] Finally, congregational divergence is not limited to Dacula and Naperville, fast-growing postindustrial enclaves outside of big cities that might be considered exceptional. As sociologist Nancy T. Ammerman concludes of a nationwide collection of congregations she studied, "In theological language, I am convinced that not every congregation is called to the same mission. In sociological language, I am convinced that there will inevitably be a wide range of responses to change . . ." (Ammerman 1997a).

The Grounds for Diversity

Instead of being part of a fixed social structure that set the religious agenda for people, as was the case for mainline religious institutions and the old middle class, local religious bodies are now immersed through social networks in religious cultures that those bodies help define and maintain but do not, and cannot, control. As this chapter has illustrated, congregations are the places in which people of a particular religious culture reembody their religious narrative. Congregations have become important places in which individuals are rerooting themselves in the social landscape that the postindustrial transformation has disordered. Religious bodies have met the particular social and religious needs of people in transitory places inundated by the stresses and challenges of life in postindustrial places. Congregations have responded intuitively to these circumstances through diverse adaptations that are religiously and socially appropriate.

In any local place, four factors extrinsic and intrinsic to congregations shape the diversity of religious bodies. Together these factors create a particular religious *niche* for the congregation. The extrinsic factors are the strength of *religious subcultures* that exist within the larger locale and the degree of *demographic uniformity* that is present within that larger community, and thus in the congregation. The intrinsic factors are *congregational form,* the shape of organizational life in which people are situated, as well as *congregational style,* the manner in which a congregation expresses itself religiously. A congregation is shaped intrinsically by the people that make up that congregation and their social contacts. It is shaped extrinsically by the religious and social character of the congregation's locale and by the character of nearby congregations. These four factors define the niche that a congregation occupies in a physical place. As congregations adapt to local change, particularly change brought on by population growth or shifts in population composition, congregations within local places not only move in diverse, rather than in uniform, directions, but they also shift to occupy new religious niches within the locality in order to stay viable.

Naturally, among physical places, the degree and type of diversity will vary. What occurs in Naperville is different from what happens in Dacula. Each town has religious and demographic characteristics that set them apart and provide different opportunities and restraints to congregations within them. Naperville has a more mainstream, if not more diverse, religious bent than Dacula, a town more given to evangelical cultures. Also, while both places are young, family oriented, and full of children, Dacula's people are more modestly educated. Naperville has more workers in professional and managerial occupations; Dacula has more workers in service, sales, and office jobs. As it is, one town is home to many of the professional class; the other is home to many of the service and technical class.[10]

For all of us, the newly arrived and the uprooted in the postindustrial world, congregations are places where we can alight and put down roots. The congregation remains the institution to which people turn to reembody religious and social narratives in a disordered society, like the Chinese immigrants described by Yang. A number of years ago, I interviewed a member of a mainline church near Washington, D.C. who struggled to explain why she had joined that congregation. Finally, she said, "It just seemed the right place for me." That is not a theologically correct answer. But the heartfelt reply is indicative of the changed role of American congregations, how they have become places that are "the right place for me."

Chapter 4

Understanding Subcultures and Uniformity

On this Sunday in August, Father John Cusick is talking about dogs. Stepping away from the lectern, he grabs four empty chairs from the choir. "The Canaanites and the Israelites treated dogs differently," Father Cusick says, placing the four chairs in a row before the packed nave. "The Canaanites let dogs into their homes, around their table. The Israelites would never do that. Dogs were unclean."

Moving behind the row of chairs, the priest tells how Matthew's story of the Canaanite woman is about building artificial boundaries, like the impromptu barrier his chairs have formed between him and the congregation. Jesus had walked along the border of despised Canaan, he says, and was accosted by the pleading mother of an ill child across the frontier. Father Cusick recites Jesus' rebuke to the Canaanite woman: "It is not fair to take the children's food and throw it to the dogs," and the woman's sharp reply, "Yes, Lord. Yet even the dogs eat the crumbs that fall from their master's table." Nevertheless, Jesus' response was to cure the daughter of the Canaanite, Father Cusick says. And by curing her, he says, Jesus crossed the line. Slipping through his barrier of chairs, Father Cusick asks the congregation, many of them young professionals living in downtown Chicago, to "cross the line" in their own lives.

West of Chicago's booming downtown, Old Saint Patrick's Church is an older Catholic parish backed up against the Kennedy Freeway. Established in the nineteenth century for Irish railroad workers, and once also the home for the craftsmen of Printer's Row, Old Saint Pat's now has a congregation that is young, educated, professional, and urbane. It is an easygoing, post-Vatican II parish whose members are interested in social issues and are active in the parish's many volunteer community ministries. Old Saint Pat's draws many of its people from nearby, newly erected residential high-rises, as well as from other

Chicago neighborhoods. The aging edifice of Old Saint Pat's has been renovated recently. The restored interior walls of the nave are patterned in intricate, handcolored wall motifs copied from the Irish Book of Kells. Atop the walls are painted statues of saints, including, of course, a towering Saint Patrick. The chancel has been reconfigured to accommodate a front altar standing on a circular, polished marble dais. Beyond the altar, the pews curve away in oscillating waves, as if a force from the altar had bent them.

This union of old and new, and of a church preserved and a church invigorated, embodies the character of Old Saint Pat's. Sociologist Elfriede Wedam, who has studied religious bodies and neighborhoods around Chicago, says this congregation of mainly young professionals is free of the hard edge of dogma and the tight confines of ethnicity that were once common to American Catholicism. No one attends Old Saint Pat's just because they have to. Unlike most Catholic churches, this church has no geographic parish. The people who came on that Sunday in August picked Old Saint Pat's instead of their own parish. In postmodern scholarship, the erosion of obligatory community and the rise of religious choice, of which the parish-picking adherents of Old Saint Pat's should be an example, is equated with the spread of religious individualism. But this congregation is not home to unleashed religious individualism. As Wedam views them, the people of Old Saint Pat's look outward religiously. They are not turned inward in the way postmodern scholars would expect. The people of Old Saint Pat's feel they are part of something much larger. Indeed, the congregants at Old Saint Pat's possess a certain sensibility, a religious sensibility that they have brought with them and that is shaping the life of the church. That religious sensibility was nurtured, as Wedam offers, "in the narratives that families pass down, and in the communities of choice in which the rituals and activities of the members help them interpret their lives and pass the stories on to others" (Wedam 2000). Old Saint Pat's is an example of how congregations have become the places in which people reestablish religious and social narratives. The tough Irish religiosity of old has been replaced by religiousness with Irish overtones. This concern for welfare of people and this awareness of a religious past are also the markers of Old Saint Pat's ties to a "mainstream" religious subculture.

In fact, ties to religious subcultures have become evident among people in local religious bodies throughout the United States. Old Saint Pat's is not an isolated example of a religious subculture, as we see in two churches, one Pentecostal and one evangelical, described below. Christ the Rock Metro Church is a small Assembly of God congregation in Dorchester, Massachusetts, a struggling neighborhood of Boston. On a wintry Wednesday night, congregants gather in a large rented house for a lengthy session of Bible study, singing, and prayer. Scattered through a large downstairs room is an ethnically mixed group of young and middle-aged couples and individuals—many of the latter are women. The children are upstairs at the Royal Rangers and Missionette meetings. Pastors Lou and Kristine Zinnanti, a young couple, double as guitarist and singer. Standing on a carpeted dais backed by a large cross, they open the Bible study with upbeat music. Pastor Lou then turns to the night's lesson in the Gospel of John. It is before Christmas, and he talks about the connection of John's gospel to Jesus' nativity. "And the Word became flesh, and dwelt among us," he reads. Emphasizing that line over and over in his Bible study, the pastor conveys to his congregants the importance of letting Jesus control their life. As Pastor Lou preaches, an intense young man with ragged hair paces animatedly at the back of the room, his eyes closed. After the Bible study, two guitarists, a keyboard player, and a drummer lead a half-hour of increasingly intense praise music. The music slowly dissolves into an emotional prayer. Speaking aloud, congregants call out the names of friends and relatives and tell of problems for which they seek solace and guidance. Everyone moves forward. Before the dais, they kneel, praying ardently, their arms swept upward.

Across the country a few days later, the Sunday night service of Mosaic Church is being held in a nightclub near downtown Los Angeles, its usual meeting place. When the club's doors finally open, a hundred or so tidily but informally dressed young people pour in and quickly fill folding chairs and long couches arranged over the dance floor. Virtually all of the congregants at the Urban Mosaic service are in their twenties, and more than half are male. The service begins with a videoclip shot by members featuring humorous renditions of the "Twelve Days of Christmas." A rock band with a slightly swaying female vocalist launches into animated praise music. Pastor Erwin McManus, older than the congregation by over a generation, turns to the first chapters of Luke to explain the meaning of Christmas: God coming into the world as Jesus. His informal talk, delivered with his Bible in hand, is accompanied by a short segment from the old *A Charlie Brown Christmas* in which Linus delivers word-for-word Luke's nativity narrative from memory. Pastor Erwin excitedly explains that Charles Schulz, the Peanuts cartoonist, was a believer, too. Like Schulz, he says, you need to share the good news about Jesus. He then leads rounds of shouting "Good News for the World," each time repeated more loudly and performed more energetically. Wrapping up the service, Pastor Erwin tells the congregation that when they go home this Christmas they should talk with their parents about faith.

These churches, and Old Saint Pat's, are examples of the diversity among American religious bodies created as they adapt to the postindustrial changes and to the particulars of their physical places. As they adapt, congregations are being shaped in four ways. The extrinsic factors that mold religious bodies are religious subcultures, like that found at Old Saint Pat's, Christ the Rock, and Urban Mosaic, and demographic uniformity, best exemplified by Mosaic, which is made up almost entirely of the young and the unattached. The intrinsic forces, congregational form and congregational style, also accentuate the diversification occurring among congregations. In this chapter, we will focus on the extrinsic forces: religious subcultures and demographic uniformity. This chapter looks at the two largest religious subcultures, as well as at the main forms of congregational uniformity.

Subcultures

Religion in America now exists within subcultures. It is not that religious subcultures were not around previously. Religious subcultures have always existed. In the past, however, they have been seen as tight groups, such as the Amish, or as inconsequential holdouts—backwoods Holy Rollers futilely hiding from the advance of modernity and alienated from the structure of society. What is present today, however, are subcultures whose presence within society is broad and substantial. The loss of stratified structure that has come about with postindustrial society, as well as the spreading ease of travel and communications, has recast religious subcultures into generalized, complex, and thriving social subsystems.

These religious subcultures are what Beyer, in his adaptation of Luhmann's theories on religion, calls *culturally particular* social subsystems. These religious subcultures are delineated from each other by social, religious, economic, and political distinctions that people within the subcultures find meaningful. These meaningful distinctions are often expressed in values, norms, beliefs, and practices. Because they are based on meaningful distinctions, subcultural boundaries are adaptive—not taut and immoveable—since meaning, while always existing, is itself adaptive within subsystems as Luhmann says. Though malleable, subcultures persist over time because they are able to draw on tradition in some form as a foundation for meaning and distinction.

Moreover, these systematic religious subcultures are broad in scope. They are not smaller "face-to-face" groups such as congregations in which people interact directly. Instead, face-to-face groups such as congregations are immersed within these broad religious subcultures through the social networks of their adherents. These congregations are also the focal points of value-based social networks, though the degree to which they serve as focal points varies. As it is, social networks are defined both by demographic homogeneity, which creates demographic uniformity within congregations, and by homogeneity in values. It is this homogeneity in values that positions congregations within particular subcultures.[1]

The Basis of Religious Subcultures

French sociologist Danièle Hervieu-Léger offers a valuable insight about subcultures. The director of the religious research center at the Advanced School of Social Science in Paris, Hervieu-Léger links tradition and subcultures. She contends that tradition, particularly religious tradition, survives through subcultures, though at times survives fragilely. Tradition also gives subcultures staying power. Hervieu-Léger says:

> The appeal to tradition and explicit reference to the continuity and authority of a shared past frequently accounts for the way voluntary groups are set up and are able to endure; and it affords a source of compensation for the looseness of current social ties. Nor is it necessary for this sense of continuity to be historically verified. It may be purely imaginary, so long as its recall is strong enough to allow identification to build and preserve the social bond in question. (Hervieu-Léger 2000)

Thus, a religious subculture uses an appeal to tradition to reinforce its boundaries, reinvigorate its symbols, and renew its identity, even if that tradition is made up. Postindustrial society represents *engagement* with tradition and not a turning away from tradition. The tradition used by systematic subcultures can be real tradition that is being maintained as it was, a real tradition that has been modified to meet present circumstances, or a tradition that has in fact been manufactured to meet present circumstances. (These terms are from Georges Balandier, a French sociologist, who, as quoted in Hervieu-Léger 2000, coins the terms as fundamental, formal, and pseudotraditionalism.) The last usage of tradition (Balandier's pseudotraditionalism) occurs in periods of rapid change and major upheaval, according to Balandier.[2] None of the three usages is more apropos to present-day society than the other. Holding onto tradition is as valid a response to the postindustrial transformation as is adjusting tradition or even inventing it.

From a Canopy to Umbrellas

Religion endures in a pluralistic society because of subcultures. When Berger wrote *The Sacred Canopy* in 1968, he was depicting an immutable moral structure—a "sacred canopy"—that protected its tenants from exposure to meaninglessness. Berger feared modernization would shred that canopy. Few scholars would accept that meaninglessness characterizes the present time, but most would agree that an all-encompassing religious motif has indeed dissolved for the United States. Instead, as Christian Smith, a sociologist at the University of North Carolina, says,

> In the modern world, religion does survive and can thrive, not in the form of "sacred canopies," but rather in the form of "sacred umbrellas." Canopies are expansive, immobile, and held up by props beyond the reach of those covered. Umbrellas, on the other hand, are small, handheld, and portable—like faith—sustaining religious worlds that modern people construct for themselves. (Smith 1998)

Religious subcultures are subsuming denominations as the foundation of religion in the United States. But denominations are still important. In spite of the growth of independent congregations and the waning appeal of denominations, loyalty to denominations remains strong among historically liturgical or ritualistic bodies (Ammerman 1999). As we saw in the discussion in chapter 3 of Beyer's conception of Luhmann's religious systems, organizations like congregations are becoming positioned within subcultures. Congregations within the same denomination may be positioned within different subcultures, and that sets up a potential for conflict within the denomination over the values inherent to those subcultures. Though their religious offerings are still valued, denominations are losing the power to gather adherents around a common understanding. As Hervieu-Léger says in a different fashion:

> The transfer of the potential for meaning vested in the historic religions from society to the individual has meant that in all advanced societies they [the religions] have become sources of cultural heritage revered for their historical significance and their emblematic function, but to all intents and purposes poorly mobilized for the production of collective meaning. (Hervieu-Léger 2000)

The Cultural Wars

Some scholars contend a brutal, polarized struggle—popularized as a "cultural war"—has erupted since the 1960s between religious conservatives on one hand, and religious liberals and the nonreligious on the other hand (Hunter 1991). These struggles are raging over such issues as abortion, gay and lesbian rights, the sanctity of marriage, and prayer in school. However, many scholars maintain that religion remains more of a cohesive force in society than a disruptive one. The actual numbers of people engaged in these cultural struggles are small: these conflicts have not energized the majority of Americans, who are not strongly persuaded by one or the other (DiMaggio, Evans, and Bryson 1996). Others have noticed that despite the supposed cultural division nationally, that cleavage is not replicated within local communities and congregations (Eiesland 2000). Some scholars do contend that society has become divided, however, and is becoming more divided on several social issues (Evans 2003). Other scholars say that a division has occurred but has reached an impasse (McConkey 2001; Smith 1998). Yet, Warner says, the course of religious change in America "is a centrifugal one of increasing complexity and decentralization. It is not, however, a picture of fragmentation or entropy. There are signs of systematization..." (Warner 1999). In fact, systematic subcultures are not naturally conflictive, though they are constantly rubbing against each other. Sometimes that creates conflict. Sometimes that creates cooperation. Postindustrial society is complex and nuanced and is not being reduced to either-or choices, as advocates of the cultural war thesis contend and the media often portray.

Pluralism Promotes Subcultures

The subcultural thesis explaining how society adapts to pluralism has been around in sociology for more than two decades. The subcultural thesis, for example, is used to explain how modernity has failed to change urban life in ways that earlier sociologists had expected (Fischer 1982; Fischer 1982; Fischer 1995). Warner touches on this subcultural thesis in his key academic article on the emerging new paradigm in the sociological study of religion (Warner 1993). A subcultural thesis has been used, too, to explain how evangelicalism exists and thrives in a pluralistic society, contrary to the contentions of earlier scholars who had held that evangelicalism would shrivel in the broad daylight of pluralism

(Smith 1999). Indeed, these scholars say that pluralism promotes the formation of subcultures. As Smith, the University of North Carolina sociologist, notes, "insofar as modernity disrupts traditional, location-based structures of community, many people seek out alternative bases upon which to construct new networks of community relations" (Smith 1998).

Types of Religious Subcultures

In depicting spiritual questors in *The Spiritual Marketplace,* Roof divided Baby Boomers into five religious subcultures based on a random survey and personal interviews (Roof 1999). Roof was using these subcultures to describe Baby Boomers, but they also describe people in general. He calls his five subcultures: Born-Again Christians, Mainstream Believers, Dogmatists, Metaphysical Believers and Seekers, and Secularists. The largest religious subculture, Born-Agains, have an identity formed around a relationship with a personal God (or Jesus) and are characterized by conservative spirituality. Born-Agains are evangelicals, charismatics, and Pentecostals. Mainstream Believers' identity is based on what they perceive to be the core cultural values and ideals of the larger culture. The second largest subculture among Boomers, Mainstreams feel they are part of a historic, continuing religiousness. A smaller group, Metaphysical Believers and Seekers include everyone from neo-Pagans to Theosophists. Similar in numbers to the latter group, Dogmatists are Protestant fundamentalists and neotraditional Catholics. Secularists rarely attend church and appear to be a-religious, but are not numerous.

The Evangelical Subculture

In his study of evangelicals, *American Evangelicalism: Embattled and Thriving,* Smith says the strength of evangelical subculture lies in its ability to maintain differences between itself and the larger world without pulling away from the larger world. Evangelical differences are based on belief. Belief is important. Evangelical beliefs focus on issues of sexual fidelity, the sanctity of marriage, strong family life, proper gender roles, and so forth. On one level, beliefs around these issues are based on what evangelicals say are the absolute truth of God's word. On another level, these beliefs resonate with what is required within the service and technical class to achieve and maintain an acceptable standard of living. These beliefs build psychological hardiness. They help double-income families stay sturdy and intact. They protect children from the corrosive effects of popular culture.

But regardless of how they are viewed, the differences that form evangelical boundaries, while widely and firmly held, are also malleable. Smith says,

> Evangelicalism appears, indeed, to construct and maintain its collective identity largely by its members drawing symbolic boundaries that create distinction between themselves and relevant outgroups. It also appears that evangelicalism strategically renegotiates its collective religious identity by reformulating the ways its constructed orthodoxy engages the changing sociocultural environment it confronts.

As scholars have noted, too, the social networks of evangelicals more often than not are tied to other evangelicals.

Evangelical subculture is anchored in tradition through its perceptions of a better but vague past. Evangelicalism sees itself as true to the nation's founding Christian principles, from which others have turned away. An interviewee in Smith's book expressed that emphatic belief: "Our nation is on the edge and falling from the true meaning of being a Christian nation." Even though evangelicalism now plays a powerful role in the religious life of the nation, evangelicals still see socially advantaged mainline faiths and the intellectual elite as oppressors. "For some, perhaps many, evangelicals, this creates the feeling of being demoted to second-class citizenship, of being suppressed by a selectively liberal mainstream that lives in denial of that oppression," Smith says. This sense of being on the defensive invigorates evangelicals, and that vigor feeds the perception that evangelical subculture is more robust than mainline subculture, which does not feel oppressed and has had no reason to mobilize people.

The Mainline Subculture

Despite perceptions to the contrary, mainline religious subculture is also strong and relevant. The sociological literature has pictured mainline religion as relativistic and accommodating and deficient in the religious fervor and devotion of its evangelical counterparts. The old sociological assumption was that postmodern society has affected mainline adherents more than it has other religious adherents. Because they were more educated and more urbane, the mainline adherents were thus being exposed to pluralism and secularization. The seeming impotence of mainline religion is cited as evidence of that. Even Smith, for example, asserts that mainline and liberal Christianity's apparent lack of clear tenets brings on "enculturation and accommodation," a condition that does not generate the religious vitality that evangelicals boast. But another sociologist, Nancy T. Ammerman of Boston University, disputes the thesis that pluralistic postmodern life has turned mainline faith into low-grade religion. Instead, she says, the basis of middle-class religion is inherently, if not historically, different from the basis of conservative religiosity (Ammerman 1997b). Golden Rule Christians, as she calls mainline Christians, "are a pervasive religious type that deserves to be understood on their own terms." "Right living" and not "right believing" is the basis of mainline religiosity.[3] Thus, the meaningful distinctions that form the boundaries of mainline religious subculture are not ideological or based on beliefs. The distinctions that are meaningful within mainline subculture are based on conventions about how people are to be treated. (Note that at Old Saint Pat's, the homily was about the treatment of people.) In surveys conducted among several mainline congregations, both Catholic and Protestant, Ammerman found, "When people of all ages talked about being dissatisfied with a church, it was rarely over doctrinal disagreements, but often over the failure of a congregation to care for someone in need." These mainline distinctions based on conventions are no less real or meaningful than the belief distinctions found in evangelical subculture. Golden Rule Christians are as sure of what a good Christian should do and in what churches ought to be engaged as evangelicals are sure about what a good Christian should believe and what churches should teach.[4]

Unlike in evangelical subculture, mainline religious subculture connects to an immediate and living past. Among Mainstream Believers, Roof says, "religious history is not unimportant; it provides continuity with kin and a level of community status most mainstream believers want to maintain" (Roof 1999). Unlike evangelicals, the social networks of mainline believers tend to be broader and connected with people of other faiths. Furthermore, the situation of mainline religiosity is not a recent development that is the result of corrosive postmodern society. The seeming impotence and languor of mainline religion is really about the fact that mainline religion has ceased to be the cultural norm in society. The class position of mainline adherents that was inherent to industrial society has faded; mainline religion cannot easily impose itself on others, though it still tries, as evangelicals complain. Yet, as a religious subculture identified with the professional class, we can contend that mainline religiosity serves its adherents well, both religiously and socially. The professional class needs to maintain open and expansive social networks,[5] to adjust to sudden job change and frequent moves, and to work with people of disparate social, religious, and personal backgrounds. These needs are more easily negotiated through mainline subculture with its emphasis on people, openness to diversity, and its reliance on historic continuity and not through evangelical subculture with its stress on belief and steadfastness in an uncertain and potentially perilous world.[6]

The Effects of Subcultures on Churches

Congregations are being captured within religious subcultures because of the social networks of their adherents. The mechanism that has brought about the capture of congregations within religious subcultures is geographic mobility. As a result of geographic mobility, people join and leave several congregations over a lifetime. As people join congregations, they gravitate through their social networks toward congregations that reflect the values of those networks. The loss of geographic ties and broad connections to physical communities has also allowed congregations to be repositioned. The capturing of a congregation within a subculture does not mean that congregants agree on every topic. It does mean they generally hold to the basic distinctions that are at the core of their respective religious subculture. Evidence of value homophily within congregations is found in survey data on denominational switching— the movement of people between churches of different denominations. As we saw in chapter 1, the greatest amount of switching occurs among bodies whose theologies are close—liberals within liberal bodies, conservatives within conservative bodies. Switching occurs less often between bodies of different theologies—liberal to conservative, or conservative to liberal (Hadaway and Marler 1993; Sherkat 2001; among many others). When people change congregations, they usually stick to congregations of the same religious subculture even if they join a congregation of another denomination. Congregations themselves can switch religious subcultures when the religious leadership changes or the congregation and its physical location is in transition (Warner 1990; Eiesland 2000).[7]

Religious subcultures have no geographic basis. But because residential places are segregated, particular subcultures are more evident in certain places. The strength and extent of a subculture locally is a restraint on local religious bodies. A mainline religious body situated in residential places where the service and technical class live is not going to flourish to the extent a mainline body surrounded by members of the professional class will. Old Saint Pat's thrives because the church can draw on mainstream believers who are plentiful and whose numbers are growing around the church.

Demographic Uniformity

Congregations in the United States are becoming more demographically uniform. Demographic uniformity is taking place because the ties of congregations to social networks are growing stronger than ties of congregations to particular geographic places. People within social networks share common social and demographic traits, as well as values. These common traits shape the demographics of congregations. Social networks are often pictured as the source of new religious converts. That social networks supply new people is also basic to the thinking of the church growth movement, as seen, for example, in the common adage, "People like to stay with their own people." The degree to which members are involved in inviting others to church, presumably from among their social networks, is related to whether a church is growing (Hadaway 1993). The emphasis here is on social networks being the source of group *affiliation*. In recent decades, social networks have become more voluntary and far flung and built less on the obligatory relationships more common in the geographic communities of the past. Social networks have become more homogeneous. Social networks are usually made up of people of similar age, family situation, education, and so forth, as well as values (McPherson, Smith-Lovin, and Cook 2001). The networks from which congregations draw their members are becoming more homogeneous and, thus, so are the congregations.

This book purposely refers to congregations as being uniform rather than homogeneous. As the term is used in church growth literature, homogenenity implies attracting similar people. With the term *uniformity*, this book is suggesting that while congregations may be made up of similar people, that situation is not coming about by their setting out to attract similar people. That situation is coming about by the way social networks and local demographics combine for a particular congregation. Demographic uniformity exists not because it is to be desired in congregations, as church growth literature suggests. It exists because uniformity is what results from the natural flow of mobile people into congregations through the established social networks of people in the congregations and because that uniformity is reinforced (but not created) through the kinds of activities, programs, and ministries that the congregations then reasonably provide.

Accelerating the process toward uniformity is the segregation of physical communities. The pool of prospective participants within reach of congregations is narrowed demographically because residential places are segregated by certain demographic characteristics. That segregation is evident in the Naperville and Dacula cases in chapter 3. Other examples of residential homogeneity are common. Around Stevenson Ranch in north Los Angeles County, for example, more than two-thirds of the 46,000 people who lived there in the 2000 Census were young parents and their children. Most were married couples. Outside of Dunellon in Marion County, Florida, about half of the 38,000 residents there were age 65 and over. Most were empty nesters. East of midtown Atlanta, Georgia, about half of 36,000 residents were young adults. Nearly all were single.

Demographic uniformity means that people within the congregation cluster around a few demographic traits, whether those traits are a particular ethnicity, age, family or parental status, education, occupational class, or others. Obviously, congregations near Stevenson Ranch are more often than usually composed of families and children; near Dunellon, retirees; and near midtown Atlanta, young singles. However, even in places with homogeneous populations, there will be congregations that are demographically different from the people living in their physical community. In these instances, adherents of those congregations are tied into social networks that are geographically far flung or connected to people who are a minority in that place. These congregations are not out of synch; they fill a needed but small niche. Some older congregations will be demographically out of synch because the niche they fill has disappeared over time.

Racial and Ethnic Uniformity

The most typical and longstanding form of uniformity is based on race and ethnicity. Race and ethnicity is a contentious issue among American religious bodies. Race has been, and still is, a theologically awkward issue grounded in the overt racism and racial animosity that historically have characterized the United States. Racism still shapes congregations. Yet, for racial and ethnic minorities, ethnically and racially based congregations have been, and still are, valuable places because they are a crucial and powerful body in which the problems of racism and prejudice can be addressed and resolved religiously and socially. But racially and ethnically defined congregations exist not only because of the particular religious and cultural needs of its members. Congregations also exist because the social networks of American religious participants still do not commonly and strongly cross over racial and ethnic lines.

Truly multiracial and multiethnic religious bodies are rare in the United States. The bodies that do exist are often Catholic churches in which diverse congregants have been tossed together because of the way parish boundaries have been drawn. Even so, the Catholic congregants may have limited contacts with each other across racial and ethnic boundaries.[8] Indeed, recent scholarly studies have shown that the survival of multiethnic congregations can be tenuous if the social networks of their participants are not themselves diverse (Emerson 2000). Congregations that are truly multiracial may be that way because of the peculiar nature of their location, founding, or membership (Wedam 2003; Emerson and Kim 2002). Moreover, the number of racially and ethnically stratified congregations is increasing because of immigration. A few immigrant congregations, however, are becoming racially rather than ethnically based. For example, several churches in the Bay area of California have cross-national Asian American memberships. These congregations are made up of young, aspiring professionals, who as it is share similar Confucian roots, but, more important, who are frustrated by social bias against Asians that hurts their careers (Jeung 2002). A few congregations do escape racial and ethnic uniformity, as evident at Urban Mosaic and Christ the Rock. (But these congregations have not escaped other types of uniformity. Christ the Rock is composed of people on the margins economically. Mosaic is largely young and single.)[9]

Age and Life Stage Uniformity

Many religious bodies are uncomfortable with the idea of forming congregations based on people of same age. The nostalgic ideal among religious bodies has been, and continues to be, for congregations to be made up of a natural range of ages. The reality of postindustrial society is that congregations are rooted in social networks and not in places. Congregations are thus formed around specific ages and not a natural range of ages. Moreover, local religious bodies are becoming increasingly composed of fewer age groups because of the demographic narrowness of social networks within congregations and the growing demographic uniformity of surrounding residential places.[10] Age uniformity is also based on life stage—where people are in their jobs, marriages, child raising, and so forth. Different life stages bring different religious needs and concerns. Because age uniformity is tied to life stage, congregations that are uniform in age are also usually uniform in marital status and family type.

Urban Mosaic is an age-based service whose attenders are nearly all educated singles and young marrieds in their twenties—a number with jobs in the entertainment industry—striving to attain a foothold in Los Angeles. Congregations like Mosaic are not based on generational culture, as commonly supposed, but are based on life stage of their adherents. The Urban Mosaic service and, indeed, the larger Sunday morning services of Mosaic Church, are gatherings of young people moving into social maturity, launching careers, and considering marriage. Few are middle-aged or older. Likewise, Old Saint Pat's is an invaluable setting for urban mainline professionals mainly in their thirties to fifties who have settled into careers, moved into marriage, and are raising children. An interesting aspect of new paradigm churches is how young the people in the churches generally are—even decades after the churches first opened their doors (Miller 1997).

A Problem with Age Uniformity

An intriguing problem arises in age-consistent congregations. People get older. They do stay at the same life stage. Unless a religious body constantly takes in adherents of the same original age, the congregation will become progressively older. Indeed, the natural tendency will be for the congregation, as its members move through life together, to gain adherents who are also progressively older. In their book on generational religion, Carroll and Roof portray a new style evangelical congregation in San Bernardino, California. Living Waters is an example of a church in which the life stage of its members has changed, and different religious needs have emerged among members. Founded to attract the young and unchurched through contemporary teaching and rock music ("Where the Flock Likes to Rock"), Living Waters has become a congregation of young marrieds, a number of whom now have children. Some members complain that the church's high-energy rock band plays *too loud*. When the study was done, the church faced a dilemma. Either the church could continue to focus on attracting new legions of young, or it could follow its members through marriage, child-raising, and so on, drawing new members from among people in later life stages. The former course meant some members might have to move on to a church more responsive to the needs of families and children. The latter course meant that Living Waters would cease to be a place for the young and unchurched, the original goal of the church. The study ended before the congregation came to a decision, however (Carroll and Roof 2002).

The Subcultural Age Gap

The average age of mainline congregants is older than that of evangelical congregants.[11] The main reason for this age difference is that these two groups are parts of subcultures with different levels of education and occupational status. The gap in age between many evangelical churches (younger) and mainline Protestant bodies (older) is often a point of lament by mainline religious leaders and scholars who suspect that the age gap means that mainline congregations have lost the young. As it is, past research has found that young mainline adherents more often permanently fall away from religious participation than evangelical ones, but that difference now appears to be fading (Healy 2003a). The gap in age is due to two factors. The first is demographic. An extensive analysis of a national survey found that the reason for the different membership trends occurring between conservative and mainline denominations is primarily because women in conservative groups have more children and have those children earlier (Hout, Greeley, and Wilde 2001). In decades past, conservative adherents switching to mainline bodies as they climbed the economic ladder made up much of that difference. The loss of that switching in recent decades is a consequence of the status mainline bodies lost when social class disintegrated in postindustrial society. Second, mainline churches are connected to the professional class, whose members require more years of education and more time to settle down occupationally. Young mainline adherents also take longer to reach social maturity (career, marriage, and child raising) and to return to religious participation. At the same time, life expectancy is greater among better educated people (AmeriStat 2002), and adherents in mainline bodies are better educated than in evangelical bodies. Not only do mainline young (who are fewer in number than their evangelical counterparts) return to religious participation at a later age (with a few dropping out), but adherents of mainline bodies appear to live the longest. The net effect of these trends is that mainline participants are older than evangelical ones.

Educational and Occupational Uniformity

Occupational and educational uniformity is another form of uniformity. This form is not necessarily the result of well-off congregants consciously excluding the less fortunate. Instead, social networks are formed around people of similar occupation and education, and religious bodies are made up of social networks. Unfortunately, a negative result of such uniformity is that people in poorly educated congregations are cut off from socially advantaged people in educated congregations. Yet, such uniformity can be helpful. Religious bodies formed of people faced with common struggles are important places in which those people can find equality and bolster themselves spirituality against the daily degradation they face. Omar M. McRoberts has found that to be the role of African American religious bodies among the poor in a Boston neighborhood. Writing about a church called Pride of Remembrance, the sociologist says the church attempts through its worship "to connect the believer with cosmic, divine forces that might enable him or her to function in the world with a sense of power and agency." Rather than being inwardly directed, however, McRoberts says that these churches sought to "catalyze social change by creating communities that instilled in individuals the virtues of equanimity, confidence, and determination" (McRoberts 2003).

Because congregations are cut loose from geographic places, social networks are the main foundations on which congregations are built. Because of the dependence of religious bodies on social networks, both religious subcultures and demographic uniformity have come to define congregations. That fact can be troublesome for some religious leaders who hold that good congregations ought to be based on physical communities and encompass spectrums of people. But nongeographic, demographically uniform congregations are also good places. Christ the Rock Church equips the working poor with the spiritual tools to endure difficult lives. Old Saint Pat's urges economically advantaged professionals to "cross the line" in their lives and to use their time and energy to help the less fortunate. Religious bodies that are positioned within religious subcultures and that are demographically uniform are vital places for their congregants.

Chapter 5

Fresh Perspectives on Form and Style

In her study of congregations and their communities across the United States, Nancy Ammerman describes two churches in Carmel, Indiana, a fast-growing suburb of Indianapolis. The first church is Carmel United Methodist, a large and flourishing mainline congregation housed in an elaborate traditional structure. The second is Northview Christian Life, a large and growing charismatic congregation housed in a simple, untraditional structure. Carmel Methodist appeals to higher-income professionals who mostly live in and around Carmel. Northview Christian attracts somewhat younger, middle-income people who are spread over the northern Indianapolis metropolitan region. Religious stability and a desire to do good are the attributes that draw Carmel's congregants to that church; expressive, vibrant worship that consoles and elevates anxious people are the qualities that draw Northview's people.

As Ammerman describes Carmel Methodist:

> Besides the worthwhile activities for their children, the worship service is the force that draws adults in. Many people mention the choir and other musical offerings as essential for setting a mood for worship. One woman talked about how she comes to worship because she needs to be "in the presence of something." Several mentioned the physical space of the sanctuary and the chapel as helping them to find some quiet, gain some perspective . . . Those who choose CUMC among the forty congregations in Carmel do so because its worship offers them a needed respite and occasional challenge.

And about Northview, she says:

> The people at Northview, like suburbanites everywhere, experience the world as a stressful place. They are distressed at the materialism that surrounds them and the busyness of life—too many things, too

much to do, too many places to go, too little time. For many, worship at Northview offers a window of calm in the midst of that busyness, a time of comfort and joy in the midst of stress. The singing, praying, and physical expressiveness of worship here help to create that sense of joy and calm and hope. (Ammerman 1997a)[1]

Carmel Methodist and Northview Christian go about worship differently in different contexts. Ammerman's description clearly places Carmel Methodist and Northview Christian more miles apart in their style than in physical distance. In the last chapter, we saw how congregations are shaped by religious subculture and demographic uniformity, factors extrinsic to religious communities. In this chapter, we see how factors intrinsic to religious communities—congregational form and style—also mold congregations. Congregational form and style are the means by which congregations create religiously and socially appropriate places that people feel are "the right place for me." Form—how the congregation functions organizationally and how people in it relate culturally—is an intrinsic element that situates congregants socially. Style is the way a congregation expresses itself religiously as it goes about its functions of worship, teaching, and even adorning its physical structure. It is an intrinsic element that situates congregants experientially.

We might think of the differences between form and style as they apply to home design. Congregational form is the floor plan of the house. The floor plan sets the size and shape of the house, the placement of the rooms, windows, and doors. Congregational style is the interior design—the wall covering, flooring, and window treatments used to finish out the house. The same floor plan can be the basis of multiple interior designs; the same finishing can be matched to different floor plans. Form is structure; style is feel.

Congregational Form

Stepping into the sanctuary and out of the warmth of an Indian summer that Sunday, parishioners are finding that the furniture had been rearranged—again. The wooden pews are formed into a semicircle. The communion table is set in the center of the room. Lying nearby is a quilted blanket to accommodate children. Still in its usual place is a large art installation—a paper tree with an array of hands and faces sprouting from its trunk as branches and leaves. In its usual place, too, is the bright stained glass on the two sidewalls, windows that date to the church's earliest years. After a lengthy passing of the peace, many announcements on church activities, and a performance by a contemporary ensemble "centering" that day's worship, the mostly white and older con-gregation—dotted with a number of male and female singles and couples and children—sings "God Has Made Me with Dignity" from the church's own hymnal. That song is later followed by two older hymns, as well as a contemporary anthem, "Holy woman, graceful giver." The commun-ion offering that day is going to a local group that assists homeless fami-lies and shelters them in local churches, including, during the past week, in this church's fellowship hall. A fundraiser is announced to support a mission trip to El Salvador. This church has deep ties to Central America. Years before, Central Baptist had hidden Salvadoran refugees in the small room which lies behind the paper tree with its upstretched hands. After the service, the congregants depart slowly, stopping in clusters to chat or talk with Marcia Bailey, the copastor who preached that day. Some have miles to go to before they reach home. In fact, few of the congregants live in this well-to-do mainline suburb of Philadelphia, though the stone church has sat on the main street between the old town bank and library since 1898.

On a pleasant fall day in Santa Ana, California, the English-speaking service at Templo Calvario is starting late. Fifteen minutes after worship was to begin, cars are still pulling into the dirt and grass parking lot behind the large warehouse that the church occupies. Other people are filtering out from the earlier Spanish-language service. Even after the service starts, people still drift into the cavernous space that serves as the worship center. Some come in from the two-story classroom com-plex that fills part of the building. Some stop to greet friends and rela-tives as they locate a seat among hundreds of folding chairs. A few are Anglo or African American. The service starts abruptly. A worship band with three female vocalists opens with a round of contemporary hymns, including the popular "Open the Eyes of My Heart." An overhead pro-jector displays the lyrics on the wall behind the band. After the music, an assistant pastor delivers a short introduction and then leads a slow-paced prayer. The prayer briefly alludes to the prolonged grocery strike going on locally in which some workers in the congregation are caught. The major part of the lengthy service this Sunday, however, is devoted to a Hispanic missionary who wants to evangelize a Berber tribe in a north African country. Dressed in that country's national costume, he tells how God wants churches to reach the Muslims. He cites biblical passages about the children of Ishmael—"fighting people"—with whom he says Muslims claim a connection. "Better send them the Word of God than send them troops," he shouts to the largely American-born assembly. Sitting to the side of the speaker is the pastor of the church, Daniel de Leon. He follows with his index finger the missionary's citations in the Bible, looking up and nodding. After a few concluding words from the pastor, the service ends as abruptly as it began and only a few minutes late. Flowing out the rear doors, families flock to their cars and slowly maneuver their way out of the packed parking lot, as still other clusters of families arrive for the early afternoon Spanish-language service.

Like the two Carmel churches, these two churches are fundamentally unalike. But not only is their worship unalike, the churches function differently and people in the congregations relate to each other differently. Central Baptist is a collegial body of about 200 members. Ties are close inside the various groups that make up the congregation. The copastors, Marcus C. Pomeroy and Marcia Bailey, bridge diverse interests within the congregation. With 6,000 attending worship every Sunday, Templo Calvario is a less tightly knit church, aside from the many ethnic and family ties within the congregation. The church leadership is zeroed in on the church's evangelistic goals. Templo Calvario has extensive educational programs and mission activities. The differences between the two churches are reflected in the worship services. At Central Baptist, the worship service nimbly embraces different constituencies—gays and lesbians, social activists, children and their parents, and more conventional liberal older members. At Templo Calvario, worship is unerringly programmed around the church's evangelical goals, even shunning local incidents, like the grocery strike.

Organizations as Culture

The idea of congregational form is rooted in developments over recent decades in the sociology of organizations known as the *new institutionalism*. These developments provide religious leaders with new and useful ways to look at congregations. The new institutionalism, or neoinstitutionalism, as it is also called, looks at an organization, such as a congregation, from the perspective of its culture and the environment in which that organization is lodged. Previously, organizational sociologists tended to see organizations essentially as rational, formal structures separated from the outside world. Business organizations, with their clear emphasis on profit, rewards, and process, were often considered the epitome of all organizations. The new institutionalism instead saw organizations as existing in a group of other similar organizations (i.e., an "institutional field"), with which those organizations regularly interact and with whose external presence they must accommodate in their internal operations. Also, the new institutionalism stresses culture—the "taken-for-granted" notions of identity and way to do things within an organization—as a basis of organizational study. The new institutionalists do not see organizational culture as an obstacle keeping institutions from achieving their goals but view culture as the means by which organizations are able to do their tasks (DiMaggio and Powell 1991).[2]

The new institutionalism is useful in understanding congregations because it is more systematic than structural. Older understandings of organizations portrayed congregations as formal structures with set norms and values that were more or less imposed on the congregants. Change came by reorganizing the congregation; that is, revamping the boards, revising the duties of leaders, and so forth to create a seemingly more workable, efficient organization, often without regard to the world outside or, for that matter, the world inside the congregation. These changes sometimes produced initial but short-term results before the congregation reverted, at least partially, to its old informal systems. With the systematic new institutionalism, we can drop this static view of congregations. Instead, we see a congregation as a dynamic organization whose core activities are complex and multifarious, a tenacious organization that resides in an unsettled environment in which the congregation acts and that acts on the congregation, and a fluid organization that accommodates and shapes congregants who, in turn, mold and sustain the organization. At the heart of such a congregation is culture: the embodied rituals, rules, and narrative that give the congregation its resilience. Moreover, this culture is thoroughly religious. This culture is shaped by an incessant aspiration for moral order, religious devotion, and social bonding. Organizational change is negotiated through the culture as the organization acknowledges changes in its environment. That environment is made up of other religious bodies, both nearby, as well as distant religious bodies to which that congregation is tied (the institutional field), and of the physical place in which the congregation is located as that place is experienced through the social networks of congregants.

Congregational Cultures

A scholarly study of congregations that has used the new institutionalism is Penny Edgell's *Congregations in Conflict*. Edgell argues that "congregations develop distinct cultures that comprise local understandings of identity and mission and that can be understood analytically as bundles of core tasks and legitimate ways of doing things" (Becker 1999).

Setting out to study congregational conflict among 23 religious bodies in suburban Chicago, she discovered distinct congregational cultures that she calls models—referred to here as forms. The congregational forms that arise in congregations are limited; Edgell identified four but contends other forms might exist. These forms are built around a set of core tasks that are inherently religious. "The core tasks of the different models are not local or idiosyncratic ideas. They are religious impera-tives broadly institutionalized in the field of American congregational religion—*religious reproduction* through worship and education, *building religious community* within the congregation, and *witness* to outsiders."

The degree to which these particular imperatives are expressed in congregations differentiate congregational forms. Though some congre-gational consultants and writers have proposed various models of con-gregations, Edgell's models should not be confused with them. The difference between what Edgell describes and what popular materials describe is that Edgell's models are based on *what is*. Edgell's models are not theological visions; they are sociological descriptions. Edgell says,

> They [the models] are not just common understandings, but they are manifest in policies and programs, in taken-for-granted ways of doing things, in sermon topics, in the interaction of members with each other and with visitors, and in the forms of liturgy and ritual, all of which fit together to provide an overall sense of identity and tenor of congrega-tional life.

Four Forms of Congregations

The four models adopted here as forms from Edgell's study are: House of Worship, Family, Community, and Leader. The popular congregational literature has used these terms, particularly "Family" and "Community," to describe certain kinds of congregations. Our use of these terms is not related to those descriptions.

House of Worship

Of all the congregational forms, the House of Worship is possibly the one religious leaders find theologically most unsatisfactory. "House of worship congregations foster the most individualistic style of religious commitment, seeing religion not as something that overlaps and rein-forces ties of fellowship, affection, and community, nor as a publicly oriented 'player' in local affairs," says Edgell. As the name suggests, the House of Worship is a congregation that considers worship its central

and most vital function. The House of Worship is also involved in religious education, community outreach, and other religious functions, but
the congregation's paramount purpose is participants' collective devo-
tional activities. This form of congregation is about intimacy, but that
intimacy is with the divine and not with fellow participants. Few
congregants are close friends, and that is fine with most people. Internal
congregational ties are weak. But people are not inhospitable.
Congregants are cordial and welcoming. The House of Worship cares
for congregants in distress. The congregation is not about tight and in-
terlocking social networks, but about being a place in which people, by
connecting to the transcendent through worship, are fortified within their
existing personal worlds. The House of Worship is not much interested
in social action or community ministry, but congregants do not see themselves as apathetic: they are frequently involved personally in a multi-
tude of community activities and concerns. Leadership in the House of
Worship is administrative. The congregation appoints or selects leaders, including the pastor, who operate with low levels of congregational
involvement. A few people make the decisions. Most congregants find
that satisfactory.

The main asset of this congregational form lies in its ability to deepen
and strengthen the religious faith of congregants who turn to religious
bodies not as places of fellowship but as places of spiritual depth. The
main liability of this form is that such congregations tend to be small—
though not always. This form is less adaptive to change, because social
networks are weakly connected within the congregation. Congregations
of this form have a hard time energizing people. Edgell says this form is
like the religious "sanctuary" that religious leaders are told from seminary on is theologically inappropriate. Yet, despite such theological mis-
givings, such congregations are vital religious centers that do important
ministry among a small segment of the populace. Houses of Worship
are not common. Only two of Edgell's 23 congregations fall into this
form. An example I have encountered was a tiny and historic church
situated in an obscure location at the edge of a metropolitan area whose
traditional rituals and rites drew people from across the city.

Family

In the Family form, the emphasis shifts from the sanctuary to the fellowship hall. Family congregations take religion seriously, but they do not
take it so seriously as to value doctrine over people. In using the term
Family to describe this form, we are not talking about congregations
made up of related people—a fading type of congregation in any case.

Nor are we talking about congregations made up of married couples with children. Instead, Edgell says, the "family" metaphor is what defines these congregations. The term "family" repeatedly shows up in the church's literature. Its members use the term "family" to describe themselves. Being a Family congregation, according to Edgell, is understood "as a feeling of belonging, a knowledge of the important events in each others' lives, and a sense of caring and support in times of crisis." These congregations are family-like places because for many people real family is neither near nor satisfactory. Solid social ties are the paramount attribute of the Family form. The time in worship given to greetings and prayers for individuals is lengthy. (In one instance, Edgell counted 90 people the pastor mentioned by name in a prayer.) The coffee hour lasts *more* than an hour. Within this form of congregation, the various social networks of congregants are more strongly linked with each other. Though these congregations are not inherently cliquish, incorporating new people is difficult. Some people find them too close for comfort; others naturally gravitate to these congregations.

An aspect of this form that stands out is how the congregation makes decisions. Decisions are felt out. Many decisions that in other religious bodies might be considered cut-and-dry are considered imminently personal in Family congregations. Family congregations try to avoid conflict. A liability of this form is that such congregations can never be large or grow much. Unfortunately, too, some pastors are never accepted as part of the family and repeatedly end up in difficulties in which they can do no right. To some religious leaders this form of congregation is contrary to denominational expectations, because this form emphasizes intimate ties over membership growth. On the other hand, given today's geographic mobility and the incessant stress of occupation and family, Family congregations create a religiously serious place where people are warm, caring, and friendly. Many people belong to religious bodies that are Families. Six of Edgell's congregations are this form. Saint James in suburban Naperville (described in chapter 3) appears to be a congregation of this form.

Community

While the focus of the House of Worship form is the sanctuary and the Family form is the fellowship hall, the focus of the Community form is the meeting room. When Edgell talks of a Community congregation, she is referring not to a congregation that is integrally part of a physical community but to one in which *being* community is the driving metaphor. The Community congregation has intimate relationships, but these relationships are within groups inside the congregation. Social networks are more linked together and overlapping than in the Family form. Yet, Community forms emphasize moral order as much as social ties. Unlike the conflict-avoiding Family form, the Community form encourages discussion but within a caring context. As Edgell explains, Community congregations strike a balance between what is right and what is caring. They struggle over religious and cultural values in an open and tolerant and not dogmatic fashion. In a process that is sometimes lengthy and time-consuming, a Community congregation seeks common ground in which the concerns of all are respected and upheld. "The religious values that these congregations express are very modern and in many ways very American. They are the values of a pluralistic democracy, emphasizing tolerance, diversity, and widespread participation in decision making," Edgell says.

Community congregations are not necessarily liberal bodies. They are all congregations that grapple with being inclusive and living out their values, as was the case in Edgell's study of a theologically conservative interracial congregation. Participants in a Community congregation are interested in a cluster of social and religious issues, but as a whole the congregation is not radical or politicized. Worship is a striking feature of a Community congregation. Because of the double emphasis within a Community congregation on finding commonality and building relationships, worship can be creative, participatory, and occasionally eclectic. The main role of a pastor is often as a facilitator who maintains the collaborative process largely conducted through lay leaders. The form has liabilities, of which the first is that important decisions require an exhaustive process. On the other hand, these congregations can be larger than Family congregations. A particular asset of these congregations is that Community congregations are vital places where people can take the values they possess, within a caring and religious atmosphere, and put them together in ways that gives their lives order and meaning. Central Baptist, whose worship is described at the start of the chapter, is an example of this form. Worship reflects the common ground achieved among different groups and participants. Community bodies are common: they made up six of the 23 congregations in Edgell's study.

Leader

Leader congregations are just that—acknowledged leaders in their locales. They take public stands on local issues that have religious implications and voice those stands as congregations in public meetings. The status of these congregations as leaders is derived not only from their vocalness; it is also derived from large memberships and from the considerable resources they are able to wield. Leader congregations are apt to engage in extensive community ministries that they themselves have established and run. Being a Leader congregation is about more than a public advocate. The particular way that congregants understand religious authority and the role of the individual in the community also distinguishes the Leader form. "Leader congregations tend to see themselves as stewards of larger traditions or values that do not spring from common congregational life or individual experience, but that have their origin outside of the preferences and needs of congregation members," Edgell says. In the Leader form, the basis of decision making is the congregation's theological doctrine, polity, and historic understandings. Interpretation falls to the congregation's religious leader, whose role is to be the faithful custodian of that doctrine, polity, and history. These basic religious values are held higher than individual values, though individual dissent is expected and respected. Still, this form curtails the role of the individual participant. But these congregations are not necessarily authoritarian, though Leader congregations can be. They have just achieved agreement about where authority ultimately lies. A Leader congregation tackles issues through a regular, routine process for gathering input, but that process focuses more on educating participants than on achieving common ground. As Edgell says, compromise is possible, but not on basic points, and what matters is not the process but the outcome. Achieving moral order is too important a goal among these congregations. (Leader congregations fall on either side of the religious divide—liberal and conservative.)

What members find meaningful in a Leader congregation is not personal relationships but that "it expresses specific social, political and religious values," Edgell says. Fewer participants have strong ties inside the congregation than do participants in Family or Community congregations. "Members of leader congregations rely on them less for feelings of intimacy and community, for fellowship and friendship," Edgell says. These congregations are not cold. It's just that friends and social contacts are optional and not the main concern of participants. In fact, Leader congregations fear that getting too involved in meeting needs of individual members would sidetrack the body from its main priorities. A Leader congregation is apt to be at the nexus of many strong social networks. Moreover, because ties are loose in these congregations, Leader congregations find it easier to grow and be big because congregants can be anonymous. Leader congregations also stress well-done, well-executed worship and have solid programs for religious education. Spiritual growth is valued but is not the primary emphasis of worship and education. The impact a Leader congregation has on the world outside is its main strength. Leader congregations can mobilize people and command resources more easily than other forms, because commitment to the congregation is based on principles and service. The weakness of the Leader form is that individuals can be left out in the cold. New members find it hard to get to know people. Regardless, Leader congregations are vital places. They provide a considerable level of moral certainty about the world and affirm the place of the individual in that world. In Edgell's study, five of the 23 congregations were Leaders. Templo Calvario appears to be a Leader congregation, as does Calvary Church in Naperville.

These forms may not be inclusive of all forms that exist within congregations today. Edgell's study was done in Oak Park, Illinois. Congregations in that well-to-do town are not typical of what might be found in other settings and in other regions of the country. Based on experience, however, as well as other sociological studies, I find those forms reflect the actual circumstances of congregations.

Congregations as They Are

A closing word about these congregational forms: these forms are based on what scholars call *ideal types*. Ideal types are not statistical models created, for example, to describe the characteristics of Midwestern Lutheran congregations with 250 or fewer members, but conceptual models based on many factors. Not all congregations fall distinctly into one ideal type or another. Many fall between. Moreover, some congregations are in transition from one type to another.[3] But viewing congregations through these ideal types, or models, more clearly illustrates the nature of congregations. We see congregations as they are. The models of congregations that are advanced in popular church material, as mentioned earlier, are shaped by theological perspectives or standards of success. We might call these models *idealized types*. These models automatically classify congregations into the good, bad, and indifferent, based on how well theological or practical goals are achieved, such as social justice or church growth. We should avoid applying such standards to the forms this chapter presents. Each form has certain strengths and weaknesses, whether the extent to which the congregations build community, foster faithfulness, do social ministry, or address moral issues. Moreover, each of these forms is a real, religiously based response to the religious and social needs of congregants and to the world outside. These forms are how religion is actually lived within American congregations. They would not exist if they were not vital to people religiously and socially.

Congregational Style

Congregational style is how religion is experienced in a congregation. Style is an important issue that many religious leaders and their congregants misunderstand. Congregational style is much more than what music is played, what instruments are used, and how worship is conducted. Congregational style is how all these elements—and others—come together in a particular way that gives a congregation its distinct feel.

The Worship Debate

Worship and music have become touchy subjects of late among pastors, religious leaders, and parishioners. A "worship war" has pitted contemporary worship with its fresh tunes, informality, and spontaneity against traditional worship with its rich sounds, splendid formality, and ancient ritual. On one hand, proponents of contemporary worship point out that congregations using contemporary music and instruments are more successful in attracting new members.[4] On the other hand, faithful and devoted adherents of traditional worship think they are being unfairly made out to be selfish sticks-in-the-mud because they value rich imagery and music. As an earlier chapter showed, traditional religious ritual and practice are important to many people. In fact, in the same surveys cited by proponents of contemporary worship are numerous examples of growing congregations with more traditional worship practices.

Appropriated Tradition

In reality, the elements of worship—music, ritual, and form—can come from anywhere and be reshaped in diverse ways as long as the result is responsive to the particular niche that a religious body occupies within its physical community. Embracing traditional worship does not just mean following what is traditional within the religious heritage of that body. Traditional can appropriate any religious heritage, as long as that appropriation is religiously proper and meaningful to the congregation. Contemporary music is not just the music that charismatic and evangelical organizations have produced, music that has strong personal and emotional qualities that are wrong for many congregations. Contemporary music can also be contemplative and community centered. Some of the music produced for use in the post-Vatican II Catholic Church is a good example of the latter type.

Ever-Evolving Worship

The concern over what happens in worship is not a new one. It has recurred throughout history among all religious faiths. Nor is the debate over what musical instruments to use—the debate over organs or acoustic keyboards—a modern-day phenomena. In the 1960s, for example, some "with it" churches thought folk songs and guitars were more relevant than hymns and organs. The nature of worship has evolved. That evolution in worship forms takes place because of social change. Social change creates new religious movements. Sociologist Mark Chaves says that new forms of worship arise because of new religious movements. As such movements come into being, he says, the way they put worship together is based on elements that people see as legitimate but also elements that help differentiate that worship from the worship of existing religious bodies. Because most existing religious bodies have worship forms that are more formal, or ceremonial, as Chaves calls them, the elements that new movements adopt tend to be more enthusiastic (Chaves 2004).

The social change brought on by the postindustrial transformation has given rise to new religious movements. These movements have impacted the service and technical class, as well as the working poor, more than the professional class. Among these classes, as a result, are found the most substantial changes in worship. Also, what is new about today's changes in worship as compared to the changes in the past is that congregations in postindustrial society have become ever more diverse, and that diversity is showing up in the multiple ways people worship. One style of worship is not necessarily displacing older styles, though newer styles are, of course, grabbing our attention because of their energy and uniqueness.

Style as Religious Expression

As I said earlier, congregational style is not just about how worship is done, what music is sung, or what instruments are played. Style can be hard to define. Sociologists try to categorize religious congregations based on their worship styles but often with mixed results because worship is complex. I contend that worship is but one element of how a congregation expresses itself religiously. Worship is the most evident and public element of that expression, but religiousness is also expressed in more private places. Congregational style is how religiousness is expressed *throughout* a congregation—in its worship, its groups, its fellowship, its Christian education, and so forth.

Three Strains of Expression

Religiousness is expressed three ways. An intensive study of congregations in Muncie, Indiana, provides a basis for understanding these three strains of expression. Muncie, disguised as "Middletown," was the setting of several important sociological studies in the twentieth century.[5] Picking up on those earlier studies, the new study concentrated on conservative congregations in Muncie. In *The Resilience of Conservative Religion*, Joseph B. Tamney describes four examples of congregations—all Protestant—that for various reasons have either resisted or adapted to modernity (or done a little of both) (Tamney 2002). He calls these congregations: Spirited, Truth, Caring, and Open (which is not a conservative church).

Spirited Church meets in an old car dealership. Its services lean to the emotional but not too far in that direction. In a good-natured way, this Methodist church emphasizes both psychological therapy and moral reform. Tamney says,

> Enthusiasm is evidenced in the lively, enjoyable praise and worship, the display of gifts, the Spirit-led pastor, and the primacy of the spiritual relationship. The church has Spirit-filled people who quite visibly display their holiness, at times coming to the altar, laughing and crying. Personal transformation is expected and encouraged by the pastoral message and by the rituals.

By contrast, Truth Church is more concerned with providing a religious environment that reinforces moral codes. This conservative Presbyterian church disdains worship as "celebration" and instead stresses worship as an act of reverence before God. As Tamney says, "Congregants are expected to immerse themselves in the life of the church and to base their lives on the Bible." Service, not therapy, characterizes Truth Church.

Caring Church promotes a therapeutic culture, but this Holiness church is less strict than churches usually are in its denomination. Eventually, Caring Church does expect people to come around morally and religiously. Until then, Caring Church remains a warm place in which people afflicted with troubles can find solace and be accepted. Notably, Caring Church's worship services are eclectic, leaning toward the spirited but with a certain reserve.

Finally, Open Church is a mainline Presbyterian church. It embraces a more liberal theology than Truth Church. Like Truth Church, service is emphasized over therapy. Like Caring Church, Open Church is accepting of difficult personal and moral situations but does not necessarily affirm those situations. Open Church conducts both a formal traditional service and an informal contemporary service, though the latter could not be described as emotional.

Different Degrees of Expression

Tamney's portraits of these churches illustrate the three strains of religious expression. First, religious practice throughout the congregation can be emotive or contemplative. Second, the congregation can expect the reform of individuals or it can expect the affirmation of individuals. Third, the congregation can be the place where distressed people are relieved of their pain, or it can be the place where somewhat sturdier people confront a distressed world. The first and third strains acknowledge the extent to which emotional worship and therapeutic religion has taken hold in many American congregations in recent decades (Wuthnow 1998). Yet, many churches embrace a contemplative religiousness and stress personal service, and that, too, is important to their participants. Spirited Church and Truth Church are examples of the first strain of religious practice. Religious practice is slightly emotive at Spirited Church but decidedly more contemplative at Truth Church. Spirited and Truth Churches are different examples of moral expectation. Individuals are reformed at Spirited Church; they are affirmed at Open Church. And finally, at Caring Church individuals are healed, but at Truth Church the emphasis is on service in the world. (Carmel Methodist, described at the beginning of this chapter, falls on the contemplative side, but Northview Christian falls on the emotive side.) These different strains fall along different points on a scale. Some churches are more emotive than others; some churches are more contemplative than others. Some churches fall in between and are basically neutral. The scales are illustrated in figure 5.1 on the following page.

The ways these three strains of religious expression come together constitute congregational style. For example, Central Baptist in Wayne, Pennsylvania, is contemplative, affirming, and serving. Templo Calvario,

Figure 5.1

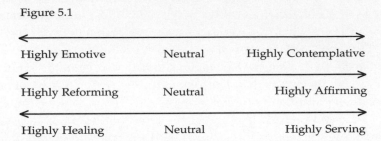

on the other hand, is emotive, reforming, and serving. The two congregations described in chapter 4, Christ the Rock in Dorchester, Massachusetts, and Mosaic in Los Angeles, are examples of how congregation style can combine the same elements to different degrees. Christ the Rock is highly emotive, reforming, and healing; Mosaic is slightly emotive, reforming, and healing.

Examples of Style

Here is how congregational style shows up in four other congregations that I visited as part of The Church in Postindustrial America project.

- When stepping through the arched neo-Gothic doors of Fourth Presbyterian Church in Chicago, one cannot miss that this church is traditional. Fourth highly values quality worship. On this Sunday in the fall, the sanctuary is decorated with artful and glittering mobiles. Like Old St. Pat's outside the Loop, this growing mainline congregation on opulent Michigan Avenue (directly across from the towering John Hancock Tower) attracts young professionals, many of them married and with young children. Since the 1960s, the church has been a dogged advocate of service to the city's underclass, particularly in Cabrini Green, an infamous project west of the church, now torn down. The church still mobilizes hundreds of volunteers to tutor the city's underprivileged school children. In its congregational style, Fourth is moderately contemplative, neutral between reform and affirmation, and highly dedicated to service.

- Tenth Presbyterian Church is a historic evangelical church set in the weathered old brownstone district of Philadelphia, now filled with students from the nearby University of Pennsylvania. Tenth, too, highly values its traditional service, with music and instrumentals performed by students of the nearby Curtis Institute of Music. Unlike Fourth, Tenth is a decidedly conservative congregation that enjoys expository preaching and solid moral expectations. Still, the congregation is also much involved in holistic outreach to the homeless and addicted. In its congregational style, Tenth is moderately contemplative, reforming, and serving.

- León de Judá occupies a remodeled commercial building in Boston. The bilingual charismatic Baptist church moved from Cambridge in order to better serve the city's underclass. Its pastor, Roberto Miranda, who holds a doctorate in literature from Harvard, delivers his sermons in both Spanish and English, slipping back and forth between the two languages. The church auditorium is packed with Hispanic congregants. The church adopted its name and moved to its present location after Reverend Miranda was spurred on to do urban ministry because of a vivid vision he had in which a gentle lion overcame a large, dark, poisonous spider looming over the Boston skyline. In style, this church leans toward the moderately emotive, reforming, and serving.

- Not far from León de Judá is St. Mark's Catholic Church in Dorchester. On Holy Family Sunday, the church slowly fills with Vietnamese families who occupy whole sections of the pews, some Caribbean immigrants, and scattered Irish couples and singles, many of them older but some young. The Vietnamese families spend several minutes in their devotions before Mass, but some of the Irish congregants, descendants of the parish's first participants, sit quietly, appearing lost in thought. A woman with a vigorous voice leads the hymns printed in the missal for that liturgical season, but many parishioners sing softly or not at all. The homily, delivered from the aisle, address issues of family life. The style here is highly contemplative, slightly affirming, and serving.

To congregants, style is how congregations become "the right place for me." Tamney tells the story of Marsha, a troubled single woman who had once attended a stern church. Marsha went to a women's retreat at Caring Church and was immediately struck by its combination of emotion, healing, and acceptance. As Tamney says of the retreat,

> The women were not solemn. They had fun. It was amazing. So much laughter and emotion. Marsha had never experienced anything like it.

People cried for each other. But it was not "emotionalism with no in-
telligence behind it." It was not like rituals when people are "not in
their right mind." It was just that the women on the retreat were being
their real selves, just as now Marsha is herself.

This chapter on congregational form and style provides ways to understand the role of congregations as they *are* in the postindustrial society, rather than focusing on how congregations *should be* in order to reach
certain goals. The chapter supplies fresh perspectives that contain an
appreciative view of congregations as dynamic, tenacious, and fluid organizations. These perspectives distance us from the contentious present-
day battles over worship and substitute a more sensitive, basic
understanding of congregations as valid variations of religious expression. These perspectives provide a solid basis from which we can understand the vital and important role that congregations play in the
postindustrial era, a subject to which I turn in the next chapter.

Chapter 6

Telling the Tale Anew

The moment had turned delicate. This congregation had been plagued by trouble throughout its existence. I was tracing that painful history, touching gently on the episodes that had befallen this body with a senseless regularity. Now mostly a handful of older people, the congregation was thinking of heeding the call of its regional denominational body to move to a growing part of the county many miles away and to start over. I had gone through the demographics of the church's present location, the demographics of prospective sites, and the plans of the county for the growing places that were fast becoming suburbs of an ever-expanding metropolitan area to the south. We had talked about the religiosity of people in those growing places.

Now the subject had turned to the congregation itself and to the attributes that the congregation possessed. It was a warm, family-like, and religiously serious body. Its history was distressing yet necessary to recall because it was unresolved. Wrinkled faces looked up at me; eyes close to tears turned toward me. Words had to be spoken carefully. Glancing up, I saw on the opposite wall a picture that had to that point escaped my attention. It was the picture of the Laughing Jesus. What in the sorrows of this church was so humorous? Was this an epiphany? Determined to get through this awkward moment, I slogged on. Months later, the church did decide to move. A new history began. Only later, though, did the epiphany from this seeming outbreak of divine levity over a church's troubled journey emerge. The message was: *Ease up. Even as they are, these people are my people. Even as it is, this church is my church.*

Earlier chapters of this book revised the well-worn script about what is supposedly happening to religion and religious institutions in the United

States. The story that replaced that script is the discovery of religious vigor by sociologists. Religion has a place in postindustrial society. Shaken by the social reverberations of the postindustrial transformation, congregations are vital and important places. They are places where people reroot themselves, where they reembody their religious and social narratives. Through the networks of their congregants and because of the changes in the postindustrial landscape, religious bodies are becoming ever more differentiated. In every place, variations in religious subculture, demographic uniformity, organizational form, and religious style set congregations apart from each other.

Having rewritten the script, this book now addresses the questions that arise from the new script. What are the main challenges that congregations and religious bodies face this century? How do religious bodies confront those challenges? This chapter describes the four challenges affecting religious institutions. These challenges are the cultural redefining of congregations because of immigration, the effects of an aging U.S. population, the altered connection of congregations to place, and the need for flexible and responsive religious leadership.

The Postindustrial Approach

Behind the central thesis of this book—that people are rerooting themselves religiously and socially in congregations after a disruptive economic transformation—is the reality that religion in the United States is more robust and congregations are more vital than popularly described. But if religion is robust and congregations are vital, the question that remains is why is life so difficult for many religious bodies? The answer we have given is that demographic forces are shaping religious institutions. I speak not of the demography of their congregational locales but of the demography of the religious institutions and religious adherents themselves. As I said earlier in the book and elaborate here, the general causes of mainline decline are not theological or organizational. The causes are the changes in fertility and marriage among mainline adherents. Mainline adherents have fewer children. Moreover, they wait to marry and have those fewer children at an older age. Evangelical and conservative adherents marry earlier, have children sooner, and have more of them. That grants those groups an edge in membership growth over the mainline. But though demographic factors are helpful to evangelical and conservative bodies, those bodies have still been unable to grow much beyond their core. Energetic as they have been, and despite the gain of many new members, the statistical evidence is that evangelical and conservative Protestants do not make up a greater proportion of the population now than they did a few decades ago (Roozen 1993). Moreover, evangelicals and conservatives are losing their demographic edge as their birth rates drop and as apostasy rates rise within those groups (Hout, Greeley, and Wilde 2001). I should add that geographic factors are also a factor among some congregations. Mainline congregations generally date to an earlier time and are more often situated in areas that have undergone the greatest, if not most continuous, disruptive demographic change (Stump 1998), unlike evangelical congregations, which are often situated in more demographically advantageous places, like growing suburbs, because they are newer.

To state that the problems of the mainline are demographic and geographic does not lighten the burden for mainline religious bodies and leaders. Those factors are as serious as, if not more serious than, the theological and organizational developments that were supposedly eroding religious bodies. The combination of demographic and geographic factors produces a frustrating predicament. That combination threatens not only the existence of many congregations, but even the existence of regional bodies of denominations. But the travail of the mainline is not endless. Demographic pressures will ease as they bottom out because births can decline only so far and childbearing can be pushed back only so long. The resulting mainline will be strong and its congregations still important in the lives of their adherents, as among all religious faiths. Though the mainline is shrinking in numbers and influence, it is not in danger of extinction.

The Four Challenges

Immigration and Congregations

Immigration and the changing ethnicity of the United States are more than demographic challenges for religious bodies. They are also social forces that are redefining congregations culturally. Religious bodies are of course interested in people's origins, the language they speak, and the religions they practice because those are factors that shape their ministry to immigrant groups. Most religious groups have in fact established new missions to attract immigrants flowing into the country. Many independent congregations have been planted, too, and new denominations have arrived from other countries.

As chapter 3 highlights, the deeper issue being brought out by immigration is not the way the nation or its religious bodies are being changed ethnically or religiously, and thus how religious bodies need to embrace new immigrant groups. The deeper issue is how religious congregations are being redefined culturally as organizations. My concern here is not what religious bodies ought to be doing about attracting immigrants and dealing with changing ethnicity but what is quietly happening to congregations as organizations as a result of immigration and changing ethnicity. Change in congregations is most evident among immigrant religious bodies. Immigrant congregations supply valuable clues about the emerging shape of congregations in postindustrial society, and indeed, immigrant congregations are probably at the vanguard of emerging changes in congregations. To learn about how to be a religious body this century, congregations and leaders need only to turn to immigrant and ethnic congregations.

Ethnic and Religious Changes

Certainly the United States is changing ethnically. At the beginning of the twentieth century about one in every eight Americans was not of European descent. At the end of the twentieth century, about one in four Americans was not white (Hobbs and Stoops 2002). Hispanic Americans now outnumber African Americans, formerly the nation's largest minority. Asian Americans are rapidly growing, though fewer in number than Hispanic Americans (Census Bureau 2004a). The number of immigrants from outside of Latin America and Asia—including from Africa and even from Europe, the historic sources of U.S. immigrants— is growing. Later this century, the proportion of non-Hispanic whites is expected to shrink to about half the population. Still, non-Hispanic whites are expected to stay the nation's largest race and ethnic category for many decades, according to Census Bureau projections (Census Bureau 2004b).

Certainly, too, the nation is becoming diverse religiously, though the United States remains largely Christian in religious practice. In a pilot survey done in preparation for a larger survey of U.S. immigrants, researchers found that nearly two-thirds of the people age 18 and over granted legal admission to the United States in 1996 were Christian. The bulk of those Christians were Catholic. Other faiths were present, too. Muslims made up 8 percent of the total response. Buddhists and Hindus each claimed 4 percent of respondents. Jews were about 3 percent of the total sample (Jasso et al. 2002). These figures indicate that the shape of religion in America this century will be decidedly Christian, despite the growing numbers of masjids and temples that dot the landscape and despite the frightful language of some religious leaders. But as

Warner notes, the point is not that Christians will continue to triumph nationally in sheer numbers over Muslims and other non-Christian faiths in spite of immigration. The point is that Christianity in this country is no longer "for European-Americans to define, speak for or even disown. Millions of new immigrants are redefining what it means to be Christian in the U.S." (Warner 2004).

Redefining Congregations Culturally

The point, too, is that immigration is subtly redefining the cultural core of congregations. The remarkable growth of immigrant religion is not leading to a melding but to the highlighting of religious particularities. For parishioners native to this country and tied to American religiousness of whatever branch, this quiet process of redefinition will in more instances push congregants toward their own histories, to reclaim and recast vague but still persistent ethnic and religious roots, than it will lead to instances in which dissimilar religious cultures are incorporated wholesale into congregations. Like immigrant congregations, indigenous bodies will be turned inward to rediscover the ethnic and religious traditions that differentiate them from each other and supply resiliency, as people reestablish their cultural and religious narratives.

For mainline bodies, which historically have laid claim to being universal in their religious faith, this redefinition may be as unwelcome institutionally as was the loss of power and status that has occurred with the dissolution of social class. But such redefinition will take place because adherents embrace it. Redefinition of a type has happened at Old Saint Pat's. Young new parishioners, regardless of ethnic background, have adopted a low-key and softened Irish religiosity as if it were their own.

Dorothy C. Bass uses an excerpt from a story about nineteenth-century Norwegian pioneers in America to illustrate how religion and heritage interact in congregations. After years of struggle in America, these pioneers finally gathered one Sunday to form a church. "Though thousands of miles from Norway, these people know what a congregation should look like, if it is to be theirs," she says. In some sense, this process is happening again, this time among native congregations. I am not saying that, as a result of this process, an old Norwegian church will be Norwegian again, much less that the Sons of Norway will be revived as an organization. I am saying that the general sense of a certain European religiousness that lives on within that congregation is the religious and social particulars that give the body its resiliency and provide its congregants the substance, no matter what are the actual backgrounds of the congregants. The particulars are the soil in which people reroot their own stories. Bass also says the particulars in a congregation call "the local leaders of congregations to place at the center of their efforts the deepening of their members' ability to participate in the practices that embody their tradition" (Bass 1998). The process of redefinition, which congregations ought to pursue, forces congregations to rearticulate their religious and cultural essence in ways that give people religious and social roots within the changed postindustrial landscape.

The Age of Aging

The second issue for religious bodies is changes in age. Those changes have many ramifications on congregations. The age structure of the United States, as well as in all countries with advanced economies, is being altered in ways new to human history. Greater longevity and lower birth rates in those nations is resulting in an age structure that is heavier on older people and lighter on young people. Moreover, the nature of old age and young adulthood is changing socially and physiologically. Old age is being postponed; young adulthood is being extended. Older adults are more physically, mentally, and emotionally agile. Because of the lengthy schooling demanded by postindustrial society, the young are delaying marriage and raising children in order to secure themselves financially and socially. The number of married couples without children at home is also growing, because parents now live many more years after their children depart. Besides the trend toward age uniformity, these demographic developments both raise questions about how age will shape future congregations and challenge the current priorities of some religious bodies.

The delays in the life cycle—that flow of life from infancy to adulthood—create two concerns for religious bodies. The first concern is that middle-aged empty nesters, who are increasing in number, attend religious services less often once their children stop taking part in religious programs. Sociologist David Roozen of the Hartford Institute for Religion Research has tracked religious attendance among empty nesters over several decades through data from the General Social Survey. His findings suggest that the attendance drop is greater among Boomers— now reaching their last years of child raising—than it was among pre-Boomers (Roozen 1996). More recent data find that Boomer attendance has not significantly slipped and may not ever (Healy 2003b).

The second concern for religious bodies is the time that elapses before youth return to religious participation as adults. A life-cycle effect well documented in the sociological literature is that youth frequently drop out of religious bodies as teenagers but return upon marriage and child rearing (Roof and Johnson 1993; Becker and Hoffmeister 2001). This time away from religious activity (but not religious belief) may be growing because marriage and childbearing are being continually postponed. This trend is more pronounced among mainline adherents because mainline young spend more time in school (being better educated) and take longer to get established (being in professions). In fact, mainline bodies have a greater proportion of people in the pews who have returned to church after time away than do conservative bodies, even though that time has become extended.[1]

At the same time, the gains in longevity may benefit mainline bodies. Longevity is greater among the educated; people within mainline subculture remain more educated than evangelicals. In fact, an explanation of why adherents of mainline religious bodies are older than their evangelical counterparts is that mainline young return at a later age and mainline members live to be older. Rather being an urgent problem that needs solving, the older age of the mainline may be, at least partly, a demographic gift.

The changes in the age profile of congregations mean that religious congregations and leaders need to turn from the popular emphasis on young generations to an emphasis on religiosity over a lifetime. Because people are living longer, the range of ages in the United States is being stretched wider and wider. But the age ranges within congregations are not always also being stretched wider. Because of the demographic homogeneity of places and social networks, local religious bodies are being tugged toward uniformity in age, as explored in chapter 4. Scholarly studies show that such age uniformity is religiously and socially useful to congregants because religious expectations and needs change with age. Different congregations will increasingly attract different ages.

Of course, worrying about the next generation is a longstanding feature of American religious life. But the programs that some mainline bodies have launched to reattract the reluctant young at a younger age or to keep them in the pews through adolescence and young adulthood, while good, may not be ultimately workable. Those programs also could be counterproductive if they alienate middle-aged and older people whose allegiance to and attendance of a particular religious body are no longer guaranteed and who are of age groups that are becoming as numerous as the young the programs hope to attract. The reality is that people remain geographically mobile. They are apt to be part of several congregations over a lifetime. That fact means that religious bodies must reattract people at several points in their lives—as young marrieds with children, in middle age as empty nesters, and in later life during retirement. People may end up each time in a congregation focused on different types of ministry and programs. That ministry and program may be specific to a particular life stage.[2]

Congregations and Places

The third issue for religious communities and their leaders is the altered ties between congregations and place. Though these changes are raising concerns among social scientists about the state of society in general, the real concern for congregations is the impact these dissolving ties have on how and with whom congregations engage in community and social ministry.

As chapter 3 explored, religious congregations are no longer linked to the places where they are located in the way they were in the past. Still, congregations "still tend to meet in *somebody's* neighborhood" (McRoberts 2003). Congregations gather in a space in a physical place. Either the congregation and its adherents are actually residents of that place, or the congregation and its adherents commute to that space and place. These are the two models of interaction that American religious bodies now have with place. In the first model, the congregation is a parish and is tied to a specific piece of earth. The second model is a commuter congregation. It is not as tied to place. The latter model is becoming more common. Unfortunately, it is easy for commuter congregations "to move their constituents to new city neighborhoods or the suburbs, depriving the old neighborhood of some of its social capital, whereas parish-based institutions are far more likely to stay as anchors in the old neighborhoods and to be ready to minister to their new residents" (Warner 1998).

For congregants and religious leaders, the response to the altered relationship of congregation to place is usually nostalgic. They sense that something that was better is lost. Yet, in physical communities, personal ties were not always voluntary and sometimes were unwelcome and stifling. Tiny wooden edifices lodged in the hamlets of the faithful are not necessarily better religiously than megachurches sprawled along the freeway. Tiny edifices locked into physical places are not always pure, ideal religious communities. They can (and did) harbor abusive clergy and parishioners—as can any type of congregation—to whom the congregant has no choice but to submit. Where ties are voluntary, as in nonphysical communities, choice is more possible: you can leave for elsewhere.

Place Is Being Weakened

Social scientists are troubled by the alterations in communities. Alterations in community change how people relate to each other. In modern society, "place becomes increasingly *phantasmagoric*: that is to say, locales are thoroughly penetrated by and shaped in terms of social influences quite distant from them. What structures the locale is not simply that which is present on the scene," notes Anthony Giddens, a British sociologist.[3] Distant ties control the lives of inhabitants in a place more than face-to-face encounters (Giddens 1990). The result is dissipating social capital, the concern voiced earlier about having unanchored congregations. Social capital is the quality and diversity of social contacts within personal networks and civic institutions. Social capital is the glue that helps stitch society together.

In *Bowling Alone*, Robert D. Putnam, a political scientist at Harvard University, raises questions about the continued ability of Americans to come together and work for the common good because, by his measures, social capital and civic participation are in decline (Putnam 2000). Many social scientists disagree with Putnam. They generally acknowledge that the nature of social relationships probably has changed but say that other kinds of associations have replaced those that Putnam claims are vanishing. For his part, Putnam categorizes civic institutions into two types. The first type of institution gathers similar people and builds solidarity through common pursuits. The second type ties together different people and groups engaged in different pursuits. The social contacts that occur in the first type are called "bonding." In the second type, they are called "bridging." The second type of institution is better at amassing social capital and encouraging civic participation than the first, but the second type is also more difficult to achieve. Moreover, the first type forges "strong" contracts and the second type creates "loose" contacts. "Bridging" is divided in two types, too. The first type of bridging reaches across racial, ethnic, religious, and similar lines. Less common, the second type reaches up and down to different positions with society, that is, the powerless with the powerful, the poor with the rich (Wuthnow 2002).

Bridging and Bonding Congregations

Putnam's argument partially revolves around whether the changed nature of religious belonging is adding to loss of social capital. Some scholars say congregations that fit the parish model are "bridging" bodies because of their ongoing contact with the places and people around them.

Other sociologists point out that most local religious bodies are engaged in a variety of outreach to other people and other civic institutions and thus are bridging, too. Some scholars say that "bonding" congregations produce social capital, too. "To the extent that congregations are providing strong, face-to-face communities, fortified by spiritual strength, they are generating social capital" (Ammerman 2002). In a study of mostly commuter churches in Dorchester, Massachusetts, it was found that those churches, strongly geared toward member needs as they were, still contributed to society. "Like parents who attempt to make a mark on the world by raising sane children, these churches tried to change the world by injecting well-adjusted individuals into it" (McRoberts 2003). Another concern is raised in a national survey of congregations that found that new local bodies engaged in "bridging" activities less often than older bodies. The reason may be either that local bodies need time to mature before engaging in bridging activities or that local bodies are in fact becoming places of bonding rather than bridging (Chaves 2002). The same researcher also contends that though congregations as an aggregate are engaged in extensive social mission, such work is only a fraction of an individual body's activity, dwarfed even by its involvement in the arts and in culture (Chaves 2004).

Shaping Social Mission

The altered ties of congregations to place are a challenge to religious bodies. But the challenge is not the role that congregations play in building social capital or enhancing civic participation. The challenge that concerns religious leaders and congregations is how to do social mission that is useful to those served. The altered ties of congregations to places raise intriguing questions about how and where congregations should go about tending to the welfare of people. These questions are made more imperative because the federal government is absolving itself of decades-old social programs and pushing them onto state and local governments, as well as religious and other charitable bodies.

The fact that religious bodies bond or bridge (if not both) shapes the social and community mission in which congregations are engaged. When they are bridging bodies, congregations can inject themselves into places, possibly bringing disparate people together to accomplish needed tasks. When they are bonding bodies, congregations can generate the internal resilience that sustains difficult community endeavors. As such, one possible model for religious bodies in community mission is to adopt a place as the basis for developing social and community mission. Another is to address particular social concerns that may or may not have relevance to any place around the congregation. The first model, which I call Garden Plots, uses the power of congregations to act as bridge among different people within a place as the basis of developing social missions; the second model, Far Fields, utilizes the power of bonding as the basis for undertaking tasks to which the congregation feels drawn, tasks that are not boundaried by place.

Garden Plots

St. Mark's Catholic Church in south Dorchester, Massachusetts, is typical of the Garden Plot model. St. Mark's is an actual parish. Once populated by devout Irish immigrants, Dorchester fell on hard times in the 1960s, much like urban neighborhoods across the United States. Except for the odd pub or shop marked by a green clover, however, this part of Dorchester is no longer Irish. It is populated by growing numbers of Vietnamese and Caribbean immigrants. New immigrant families occupy the tall triple-decker homes—as they are called in Dorchester—that once housed on different floors three extended families. Many of St. Mark's parishioners are again immigrants and their descendants. Several years ago, St. Mark's decided to commit itself to the problems of its parish population, regardless of religious background, according to its pastor, Father Dan Finn.[4] The church even dropped its religious educator post to hire a community organizer who was Baptist. The parish periodically sounds out the needs of its neighbors through forums. Those forums have led to engagement in many community activities, from organizing neighborhood watches to teaching English to training local leaders. The blocks around St. Mark's have staunchly resisted much of the poverty and crime that have infected other parts of Dorchester. The efforts of St. Mark's have helped to maintain the neighborhood's tenacity and restrain the forces that were eroding its old ethnic cohesion and driving it economically downward.

The Garden Plot model does not mean that a religious body must focus on its own locale. Not all nearby people are as needy as those around St. Mark's. Congregations can adopt places other than where they are located. In that adopted place, they can involve residents and embark on social mission appropriate to that place and those people, either alone or in cooperation with other congregations. As well as bridging across race and economic lines, the congregation becomes a source for needed volunteers, helpful resources, and relevant information, if not needed political and social influence.

Far Fields

Central Baptist Church of Wayne, Pennsylvania, is a good example of the Far Fields model, although the church also has some place-based ministries. Located in a well-to-do mainline town outside of Philadelphia, the church is engaged in homeless ministry and advocacy, among other missions directed toward social change. Through the Interfaith Hospitality Network of the Mainline, Central occasionally shelters homeless families and single women. It participates in and gives extensively to homeless organizations. Typical of the intensive activities directed toward social change is the ecology task group. It has called on state politicians, signed state and national resolutions, and helped organize a Philadelphia earth summit. The church donates a large part of its mission money to county- and city-wide programs devoted to addressing racism and prejudice against gays and lesbians and participates in related organizations.

The Far Fields model is not restricted to liberal mainline congregations, which Central Baptist is. Templo Calvario of Santa Ana, California, also addresses broader issues of hunger by using its large warehouse and huge walk-in cold storage as the collection point for donated foodstuffs that are distributed to food pantries and community programs around Orange County. León de Judá of Boston, the charismatic Baptist church, engages in a Christian arts ministry in the larger Boston community. In these cases, the issues lack the tight spatial focus of parishes or congregations in the Garden Plots model. The congregation also may use its religious resiliency—derived from bonding—to take on tasks that, in at least some cases, because of the unstructured and seemingly headless nature of postindustrial society, may require great effort to sustain.

Postindustrial Leadership

The fourth issue is religious leadership. The role of ordained and lay leaders within congregations is the subject of considerable discussion today within religious bodies, theological schools, and congregational literature. That discussion is as earnest as the discussion within corporations, business colleges, and management literature about the appropriate role of business leaders today.

As discussed in chapter 2, management methods and work regimes in businesses have been dramatically altered. New ideas of management developed for business organizations have also become the source of management models in congregations, as well as in national and regional religious bodies. Some religious bodies have adopted in some form the work teams, flexible management, and information technology used in present-day corporations. It is not surprising for religious bodies to adopt ideas from businesses. Many American denominations erected large bureaucratic structures and developed professional hierarchies in the early twentieth century like those found in industrial corporations (Weeks 1992). Theologian H. Richard Niebuhr laid the basis for professionalized ministry, for what Niebuhr called the "pastoral director" of congregations (Niebuhr 1956). Perhaps even wistfully, scholars have pointed out that it was churches and their nineteenth century missionary associations that had supplied the organizational skills that made the development of the modern corporation possible (Richey 1994). Even today, as scholars have noted, ideas are still traded between business and religious bodies. The present-day emphasis in business leadership on vision, vision statements, and visionary leadership utilizes a word whose meaning comes from religious communities. That word has found its way back into religious bodies from businesses, this time with a meaning that speaks more about deliberate organizational direction than of religious prophecies.

Looking Inside for Leadership Models

The role of religious leadership appears to be at a juncture similar to that which occurred during the height of industrialism when Niebuhr published his book on ministry. The changing role of religious leadership is a constant theme in the congregational literature today. Lyle Schaller in his previously mentioned book devotes more than 60 pages to the topic. Much of the congregational literature calls for entrepreneurial or servant leadership similar to what is found in many trend-setting companies and in emergent new paradigm churches and megachurches (Sargeant 2000; Miller 1997). Though the instinct to borrow from business is strong, and often appropriate, this time around religious bodies ought to look inside themselves for models of leadership. As noted earlier, religious bodies are much more complex than business organizations because congregations are voluntary bodies linked to the transcendent. Also, and unlike businesses, congregations are at the nexus of social networks and are thus plugged into the world around them in ways that business organizations cannot be. Businesses are exposed to a changing market environment in the global postindustrial economy. Distant events, financial trends, and product changes can suddenly reduce profits—or vice versa. Congregations exist within the less stormy waters of their religious subcultures and demographic constituencies.

Flexible and Responsive Leadership

Leadership is a broad topic. The issue cannot be explored in detail in this space. But generally, chapter 5 raises two key points in its discussion of congregational form that should be addressed here. The chapter reinforces the idea that we need to understand congregations and leadership differently. The new institutionalism supplies a cultural and systematic understanding of congregations that suggests that good, vision-driven congregational leaders should be, above all, deliberate and observant. Religious leaders should be organizationally flexible and personally responsive to a variety of congregational situations and local circumstances that are present in postindustrial society. We saw in chapter 5 that congregations have different forms, and different religious leaders are needed for those different forms. Those forms also have different patterns of lay participation. The House of Worship form had leadership that was administrative, backed by a small but dedicated core of volunteers. Religious leaders in the Family form were either part of the congregational "family" or sat outside it. In the Community form, the religious leader acted as a facilitator, collaborating with divergent groups of congregants. The Leader form, as its name implies, is a more iconoclastic version of religious organization. The Leader congregation is usually more formally organized and headed by a strong leader whose authority rests on religious heritage or doctrinal interpretation. Obviously, it is not possible for a pastor or rabbi to lead a Family congregation using a leadership style that is workable in a Leader congregation. No matter how effective a leader that pastor or rabbi was in a previous congregation, for that leader to switch to a congregation of a different form, he or she must be ready to engage the congregation on the basis of its longstanding form and leadership patterns. Otherwise, the leader faces a nearly insurmountable obstacle to effective leadership.

The exception to this rule is when a congregation is in transition from one form to another because of intensive demographic and religious changes in its place. In that situation, the religious leader must be able to bridge both forms and both leadership types and move with the direction of the congregation. An example that appeared earlier in the book is the case of Wheatland-Salem Church in Naperville. That church went from a rural, tight-knit congregation to a looser knit, suburban congregation as nearby farms disappeared and tract housing appeared.

Differences in congregational form suggest that theological schools and ministerial programs need to train leaders who fit a range of situations, rather than embrace a single style of leadership. Also, congregations calling new leadership and regional religious bodies placing new leadership need to be attuned to the types of leadership styles that are workable in different congregations.

Entrepreneurials Need Not Apply

Second, the entrepreneurial, risk-taking, innovative leadership that has gained so much notice in the management and congregational literature has a place in the postindustrial congregation, but not always. The social networks that underpin a congregation can threaten the longevity of a congregation if those networks become closed up. In such cases, entrepreneurial leadership is key because congregations then need to link to new networks in order to survive. In Dacula, a rural church with closed-up networks was unable to adjust and died, while another congregation grew into a megachurch because an entrepreneurial leader was able to tie the body to the emerging social networks of recently arrived residents. Entrepreneurial leaders bring the possibility of new people and new ministry.

But for congregations whose social networks are solidly anchored in less fluid places, entrepreneurial leaders can be dysfunctional. They can be dysfunctional especially when such leadership has set, preconceived ideas of how the religious body must function that do not fit the niche in which the congregation is lodged, threatening the very basis of the congregation, or that needlessly cuts across the congregational form and style of the body, setting off potentially unresolvable conflict within the congregation. Still, in some congregational literature, such leadership is celebrated as "transformative" because it plows over the real objections of faithful congregants who, as conventional wisdom has it, must be out of touch. An example of what can go wrong is found in a news release a few years ago from a church transformation conference. The release highlighted the story of a supposedly courageous pastor who, doggedly outmaneuvering his congregation's aged members, moved the well-established mainline church into an old movie theater and radically changed the worship style in order to better attract younger people. The fact that many older members left was seen as the redemptive of the pastor's clear vision and entrepreneurial spirit. The release (I won't mention the source) failed to note that the church was in a well-known Sunbelt *retirement* town with preciously few young people.[5]

The key to good leadership in the postindustrial congregation, regardless of congregational form, is through deliberate process, careful listening, and intimate work with the congregation. None of this is to say that congregations are always right or always are run well. After all, congregations are made up of humans. But they are religiously faithful humans, however vague that may be, who have voluntarily associated with and freely devoted themselves to that body. Religious leaders have no reason to believe that congregations are somehow more imperfect than other human institutions.

Changing Course

Throughout the book, I have suggested that the bold and transformative remedies that some leaders and congregants have embraced are not necessarily appropriate because they are based on outdated theories and misplaced fears. Radically transforming congregations will not resolve the demographic and geographic problems that face religious bodies. Worse, radically transforming congregations to conform to idealized conceptions or to embrace narrow models of success can strip congregations of the particulars that have made them vital places to people in the postindustrial transformation. I have also presented newer sociological interpretations of the present-day society and religion that suggest different courses. Newer academic studies have found, too, that in the United States religion is vigorous and religious communities are vital. With fresh eyes, the sociological community has revisited congregations and come away with a new story. It is time that religious leaders and religious institutions acquire fresh eyes, too, and see that the story of religion in America and of religious communities is not following the same old script. The future of religious communities is good. It is time to turn course.

Ease up. Even as they are, these people are my people. Even as it is, this church is my church.

Notes

Preface

1. The quote is from *Congregations in Conflict: Cultural Models of Local Religious Life* (Becker 1999). Since that book was printed, the author has reverted to the name of Penny Edgell and dropped the name Becker. In this book, she will be referred to as Edgell but listed in citations as Becker to conform with the name used in the publication.

Chapter 1

1. James F. Hopewell, then a professor at Candler School of Theology, described in a 1982 article in the *Christian Century* how, by the 1970s, local congregations were being cast as monstrous (Hopewell 1982).

2. Despite its name, "rational choice" theory does not suggest that people make rational decisions about religion.

3. Hopewell of the Candler School of Theology also wrote *Congregation* about a church, published by Fortress Press in 1987.

4. Sociologists also refer to our present time as high modernity, late modernity, or ultra-modernity. A few persist in calling it modernity. British sociologist Anthony Giddens suggests "radicalized modernity" (Giddens 1990).

5. See, for example, *New Seeds of Contemplation*, originally published in 1961 by New Directions and republished in 1974 by W.W. Norton & Company, New York.

6. In the 1988–1991 and 1998 General Social Survey, respondents

were asked about what makes a good Christian or Jew. Five levels of response from very important to not very important were listed. On the question of about regular attendance, in 1998, 44% picked the top two levels, ranking it as highly important to them, and 36% picked the lowest two levels, indicating that it was not that important to them. In 1988–1991, the results were similar, 43% and 35%, respectively. On the second question about following teachings, in 1998, 54% picked in the top two responses and 23% picked the bottom two. In 1988–1991, the results were 57% and 23%, respectively.

7. These academic research findings may seem surprising in face of the considerable religious literature being produced over purported generational gaps. There has been a myopic view that if generational gaps existed because of Baby Boomers, than important and critical gaps must exist among all generations. This is not so. The reality is that generational culture is fragile and does not occur with every age of people. Indeed, much of the study into generations by these consultants and nonscientific researchers is based on unusually thin, if not bad, data and contains conclusions that sometimes are more speculative than are supported by the data.

8. With 4.0 being the highest score on their individualism scale, pre-Boomers scored 2.8, Boomers scored 3.0, and GenXers scored 3.3. The differences are statistically significant.

9. The one academic evaluation by a sociologist of religion is of church growth consultations. C. Kirk Hadaway, now a researcher for the Episcopal Church, found that the consultations had an impact on congregations but that impact substantially dwindled a year later. Hadaway said that the consultations initially created enthusiasm and activity. That excited members, who then invited friends to church. But the enthusiasm and activity waned and programmatic changes fell apart (Hadaway 1993). The assumption to be made from this study is that it is not the program itself that brings growth and vitality but the fact the congregation is engaged in a program that brings growth and vitality.

10. I am indebted to Matthew Price and his article "After the Revolution: A Review of Mainline Protestant Clergy Leadership Literature Since the 1960s" in *Theology Today* for identifying these two works (Price 2002).

Chapter 2

1. Employment in goods-producing industries in the United States peaked at about 24.2 million in 1970. According to the federal Bureau of Labor Statistics, 16.7 million people worked in manufacturing in 2002. But the value of products went from $1.4 trillion in 1977 to $3.8 trillion in 1997, based on the Economic Censuses for those years. In 2000, 49.7 million Americans had service jobs and 19.9 million worked in manufacturing, according to the bureau.

2. U.S. educational levels have risen sharply as a result. Since 1970, the peak year of industrial employment, and 2002, the number of Americans age 25 and over who had only an eighth-grade education fell 58%, and the number with four years or more of college rose 304%. The number with some postsecondary school education was up 312%.

3. Seminary trained pastors are among those feeling the salary pressure on professionals. Researchers Becky R. McMillan and Matthew J. Price at Duke University have documented how most pastors have been pushed out of the middle range in income because of low salaries (McMillan and Price 2003).

4. Ruth Buchanan, writing in *Laboring Below the Line*, describes Cindy, a 23-year-old New Brunswick, Canada, woman who works at a call center for $8.00 an hour. Taking no longer than 150 seconds per call, she handles several hundred callers a day, a number of whom are irate. Cindy has a degree in marine biology (Buchanan 2002). Katherine S. Newman, a social scientist at Harvard University, describes the downward trend in occupations in *Falling from Grace: Downward Mobility in the Age of Affluence* (Berkeley, Calif.: University of California Press, 1999).

5. A Brookings Institution report issued in May 2003 noted a sharp decline in areas of concentrated poverty in the United States over the past two decades, except in some western cities and in inner suburbs (Jargowsky 2003).

6. Much of the description of the new nature of work that follows is drawn from "New Forms of Work Organization" (Smith 1997).

7. Another term is "edge city," popularized by journalist Joel Garreau in *Edge City: Life on the New Frontier* (New York:

Doubleday, 1991) to describe suburban office centers and adjoining malls. But nodules are not cities. They lack the mix of residential and business services that characterize a true city. Garreau's edge cities are a version of a nodule.

8. In place of our functional portrayal of the city, other scholars see recent changes in urban geography as being akin to the development of theme parks. Their largely descriptive understanding of the city stresses the consumerist aspects of urban geography—the spread of shopping malls, for example, and the chaotic way urban configurations are occurring. These scholars include Michael Sorkin, an architect who teaches at Cooper Union and Yale University, and Michael J. Dear, a geographer at the University of Southern California (Sorkin 2000; Dear 2002).

9. The data is from the Census Bureau's 2001 Current Population Survey. That survey had a larger sample and different methodology than previous surveys. The mobility rates in that survey are lower than in previous surveys.

10. The sexist nature of the question is based on the fact that, for most respondents, it was their father who held a career job, not their mother, another indication of how much things have changed over the past couple of decades. The respondents, however, are both male and female.

11. This is what sociologists call a cultural materialist perspective. In its original form, however, cultural materialism was used by anthropologist Marvin Harris to explain religious belief, such as why Hindus hold cows as sacred. The broader perspective presented here is as the theory has been adapted by later scholarship.

Chapter 3

1. Not all scholars agree that assimilation has been diminished. For example, Richard Alba of the State University of New York at Albany says that while assimilation has changed, it is still taking place (Alba and Nee 2003).

2. The idea of melting pot had religious overtones. The term is from a popular Broadway play in 1909, *The Melting Pot*, written by British-born playwright and religious leader Israel Zangwill. The update of Shakespeare's *Romeo and Juliet* has feuding Jew-

ish and Cossack families laying aside ancient hatreds for a young couple. In the play is the line: "America is the crucible of God. It is the melting pot where all the races are fusing and reforming . . . these are the fires of God you've come to. . . . Into the crucible with you all. God is making the American."

3. The number of foreign-born persons in the United States reached an all-time high in 2002: 32.5 million people, or 11.5% of the population (Schmidley 2003). In 1970, the number stood at 9.7 million, or 5.4% of the population.

4. Just as he did for the study of congregations, Stephen Warner has also been instrumental in the study of immigrant congregations. His New Ethnic and Immigrant Congregations Project was the first attempt to look a broad cross-section of American immigrant religious bodies. This research was followed by similar projects throughout the United States, including Chicago, Houston, Los Angeles, and New York, that have provided a wealth of information about immigrant religious bodies. A number of the studies resulting from those projects are cited in this chapter.

5. I am indebted to Dorothy C. Bass and her discussion of how the ideas of philosopher Alasdair MacIntyre apply to congregations for the word *reembody* (Bass 1998).

6. The articles include "Stressed Out in Suburbia" in the November 1989 *Atlantic* magazine and "Technoburb" in the January 1993 *Inland Architect*. *Everyday Revolutionaries: Working Women and the Transformation of American Life* is a journalistic account by Sally Helgesen of the life of working women in Naperville (New York: Doubleday, 1998).

7. Donald Miller, a sociologist at the University of Southern California, says that new paradigm churches are a "second reformation that is transforming the way Christianity will be expressed in the new millennium." With echoes of Gibson Winter, he foresees of mainline churches: "Huge edifices will remain on many major street corners of America, but their endowments will barely support their physical maintenance."

8. In addition to Numrich's study, I have toured Naperville and collected additional data. Other than that done by Numrich, however, I did no fieldwork or visits in these congregations.

9. But even as congregations have addressed the needs of

Naperville's residents, Numrich notes that those bodies are unable to do anything about the underlying causes of those needs, underscoring one of the dilemmas of postindustrial society. "The case studies presented in this chapter suggest that congregations in edge-city technoburban milieus may tend to offer spiritual palliatives for individuals rather than structural alternatives." I disagree. It's not that the congregations are ineffective, or even superficial, in their ministry now; they can and do effectively help people and communities. But the conditions in which they do ministry are different.

10. The demographic comparison is from the 2000 Census, which was taken after Numrich and Eiesland conducted their studies. The Naperville data is for the township; the Dacula data is for the Dacula-Rocky Creek CCD. Over half of Naperville adults had a four-year or advanced college degrees, more than twice the proportion in Dacula. Over half of Naperville's workers had professional and managerial jobs; about two-fifths of Dacula's workers had service, or sales and office occupations, slightly more than the proportion with managerial and professional jobs. Noteworthy is that in both places over half the population did not live there five years ago.

Chapter 4

1. A good summary of the sociological literature on network homophily is "Birds of a Feather: Homophily in Social Networks," published in the *Annual Review of Sociology* (McPherson, Smith-Lovin, and Cook 2001).

2. The excerpts provided by Hervieu-Léger are from *Le Désordre: Élogue du mouvement,* published in 1988 by Fayard, Paris. The entire book has not been translated into English.

3. Linda Woodhead of Lancaster University, a British scholar who studying religion in the town of Kendal, says that mainline believers have a "humanized" religion. "What matters for humanized Christians is not believing the right things so much as doing the right things. And the right things are those that help one's fellow human beings and improve one's community and society. Thus the human is divinized, and the divine humanized" (Woodhead 2003).

4. To the despair of religious leaders, and unlike their evangelical counterparts, Golden Rule Christians are often not religiously learned. As Ammerman notes, mainline adherents do not articulate their beliefs easily; those beliefs are more unspoken than explicit.

5. Conservative adherents, being more often members of religious sects, usually have social networks that are nearly completely within their religious group, with fewer contacts outside the group (Iannaccone 1988).

6. Sociologist James Davison Hunter has also investigated the role of religion within what he calls the "New Class" of professionals and among evangelicals outside that highly educated class (Hunter 1983). While his arguments are similar in some respects to mine, the conclusions that he presents are much different than those reached in this discussion.

7. Nancy L. Eiesland's study of Dacula, Georgia, includes a church that changed religious subculture. The bishop assigned to the church a pastor that the bishop hoped would help the church grow. The pastor turned out to be a charismatic. Into this church, mainly made up of people like Roof's Mainstream Believers, poured Born-Agains, who took over leadership, replaced the choir, and decided that a statue of Jesus in the church parlor was idolatrous. Many older members dropped out. "We just quit going," said one. "I don't miss the clapping of hands and almost jumping over the pews and all that." The bishop later dismissed the pastor, and the charismatic members left (Eiesland 2000).

8. In a random national survey of congregations, 8% of congregations were identified as "mixed," that is, having 20% of their adherents being of another race or ethnicity. The figure was 20% among Catholic parishes. Based on a sample of 488 congregations, the survey for the Multiracial Congregations Project was conducted in 1999–2000.

9. Patricia Dorsey describes a diverse Assembly of God church in Houston made up of people of 48 nationalities. Even in this church, however, people are mostly of a few ethnicities: Anglos, Nigerians, Filipinos, and Hispanics. Some have their own separate groups or worship services; some are even cliquish (Ebaugh and Chafetz 2000).

10. In the National Congregations Survey conducted in 1998 of leaders in 1,236 congregations, the age consistency of congregations is apparent. Despite that about 24% of the U.S. population in 2000 was between ages 18 and 34, in about half of congregations, that age made up more than a quarter of their congregation. One in 10 congregations had that age group make up more than half of congregants. Likewise, more than two-fifths of congregations had people age 60 and over make up a quarter or more of the congregation, though that age was about 16% of the population in the 2000 Census. About one in seven congregations had age 60 and over individuals make up over half of congregants. Having out-sized proportions of an age group appears to be common among American congregations.

11. In the National Congregations Survey, 39% of religious bodies, which the leader identified as more conservative, had an estimated 26% of its adherents age 65 and over, and 52% had 26% of its adherents age 18 to 35. Among congregations identified as more liberal, the percentages were 45% and 41%, respectively.

Chapter 5

1. And also a new-paradigm church that incorporates traditional elements. Ammerman describes the Northview's intinction communion and notes, "The pastor is also intent on introducing other practices and symbols from the larger church community, infusing them with new meaning as they are practiced in this charismatic congregation."

2. The "The Iron Cage Revisited," an academic article these scholars jointly authored, has a particular pertinence to religious organizations. DiMaggio and Powell noted the tendency of organizations, when faced with change, to adopt solutions from other organizations in their field ("institutional isomorphism") regardless of whether or not the adopted solution was actually producing worthwhile results in the other organizations (DiMaggio and Powell 1983).

3. Edgell found that a shift from one congregational form to another to be the basis of continuing, nearly unresolvable conflict in a congregation. The congregation is essentially swapping one culture for another. Participants find it difficult to cross over that cultural divide. As a longtime member told her about a

newly emergent group in a badly conflicted Oak Park congregation: "I wasn't going to the same church they were."

4. In the Faith Communities Today survey, conducted of congregational leaders across several faith groups in 2000, a stress on "uplifting inspirational worship" led to strong growth among Protestant bodies, as did the use of an electronic keyboard, regardless of theological tradition (Dudley and Roozen 2001).

5. These earlier studies were done by Robert and Helen Lynd, who pioneered the use of social surveys. The first study was in 1924 and the second in 1935. The Lynds looked at a range of community issues, including social class and religion. In the 1970s, Theodore Caplow and his colleagues did a third sociological portrait of Middletown.

Chapter 6

1. In the U.S. Congregational Life Survey, conducted of attenders at 2,000 congregations in 2001, a third of the people who attended a mainline Protestant church less than five years were "returnees"—coming back after an absence—compared to 16% of conservative Protestant and 20% of Catholic new attenders. New attenders were more common among conservative congregations, and more of them had recently attended a church of a different denomination (40%) than mainline (25%) and Catholic (11%) new attenders (Woolever 2002).

2. In his historical study of a New England congregation over three centuries, Harry S. Stout of Yale University and colleague Catherine Brekus of the University of Chicago Divinity School, found that between 1680 and 1700, half of Center Church's male converts were over age 30, then well into adulthood. The new members were generally the offspring of longtime members and lived in a culture that demanded that its young profess (Stout and Brekus 1998).

3. Anthony Giddens offers an explanation of modernity that seems similar to the postindustrial explanation set forth in this book. The explanations are not entirely similar. For example, his concept of "reembedding" is not the process described in this book as "reembodiment." Reembedding is the ability of individuals in a global modern society to reappropriate fragments of social

contexts across time and place. Reembodiment is the subcultural process by which institutions through individuals reestablish cultural narratives, even if imaginary or greatly revised.

4. The effort in its parish paid off in another way for St. Mark's. In May 2004, St. Mark's escaped the closures that befell 60 parishes in the Archdiocese of Boston, including parishes in and around Dorchester (Tracy 2004).

5. The prospect that religious leadership may become more abusive organizationally is unfortunately strong. An extensive study of seminary and rabbinical students in 2001 raised serious questions about whether the quality and psychological profile of students were declining (Wheeler 2001). Another extensive study has raised troubling concerns about the effects on future conduct of the sadly low salaries that await many seminary graduates. The need for more money may drive pastoral decisions instead of their religious calling (McMillan and Price 2003).

Bibliography

Alba, Richard, and Victor Nee. *Remaking the American Mainstream: Assimilation and Contemporary Immigration*. Cambridge, Mass.: Harvard University Press, 2003.

AmeriStat. "Higher Education Means Lower Mortality Rates." Washington, D.C.: Population Reference Bureau, August 2002.

Ammerman, Nancy T. *Baptist Battles: Social Change and Religious Conflict in the Southern Baptist Convention*. New Brunswick, N.J.: Rutgers University Press, 1990.

———. *Congregation and Community*. New Brunswick, N.J.: Rutgers University Press, 1997a.

———. "Connecting Mainline Protestant Churches with Public Life." In *The Quiet Hand of God*. Edited by Robert Wuthnow and John H. Evans. Berkeley, Calif.: University of California Press, 2002.

———. "Golden Rule Christianity: Lived Religion in the American Mainstream." In *Lived Religion in America*. Edited by David Hall. Princeton, N.J.: Princeton University Press, 1997b.

———. "New Life for Denominationalism." *Christian Century* (March 15, 2000): 303–7.

———. "Postmodern Trends in Religious Organizations." Paper presented to the annual meeting of the American Sociological Society and the Association for Sociology of Religion, Chicago, August 1999.

Anderson, Sarah E., Gerald E. Dallal, and Aviva Must. "Relative Weight and Race Influence Average Age at Menarche: Results From Two Nationally Representative Surveys of U.S. Girls Studied 25 Years Apart." *Pediatrics* 111 (April 2003): 844–50.

Bachu, Amara, and Martin O'Connell. *Fertility of American Women: June 2000*. Current Population Reports. U.S. Census Bureau. Washington, D.C.: Government Printing Office, 2001.

Bass, Dorothy C. "Congregations and the Bearing of Traditions." In *American Congregations.* Vol. 2, *New Perspectives in the Study of Congregations.* Edited by James P. Wind and James W. Lewis. Chicago: University of Chicago Press, 1998.

Becker, Penny Edgell. *Congregations in Conflict: Cultural Models of Local Religious Life.* New York: Cambridge University Press, 1999.

Becker, Penny Edgell, and Heather Hofmeister. "Work, Family, and Religious Involvement for Men and Women." *Journal for the Scientific Study of the Religion* 40 (December 2001): 707–22.

Bell, Daniel. *The Coming of the Post-Industrial Society: A Venture in Social Forecasting.* New foreword ed. New York: Basic Books, 1999.

Bellah, Robert N., Richard Madsen, William M. Sullivan, Ann Swidler, and Steven M. Tipton. *Habits of the Heart: Individualism and Commitment in American Life.* New York: Harper & Row, 1986.

Berger, Peter L. "Protestantism and the Quest for Certainty." *Christian Century* (August 26, 1998).

———. "Reflections on the Sociology of Religion." *Sociology of Religion* 62 (Winter 2001): 443–54.

———. *The Sacred Canopy: Elements of a Sociological Theory of Religion.* New York: Anchor Books, 1969.

Beyer, Peter. *Religion and Globalization.* London: Sage Publications, 1994.

Bibby, Reginald W. "On Boundaries, Gates, and Circulating Saints: A Longitudinal Look at Loyalty and Loss." *Review of Religious Research* 41 (December 1999): 149–64.

Boyer, Paschal. *The Naturalness of Religious Ideas: A Cognitive Theory of Religion.* Berkeley, Calif.: University of California Press, 1994.

Buchanan, Ruth. "Lives on the Line: Low Wage Work in the Teleservice Economy." In *Laboring Below the Line: The Ethnography of Poverty, Low-Wage Work, and Survival in the Global Economy.* Edited by Frank Munger. New York: Russell Sage Foundation, 2002.

Burtless, Gary. *Effects of Growing Wage Disparities and Changing Family Composition on the U.S. Income Distribution.* CSED Working Paper No. 4. Washington, D.C.: Brookings Institution, July 1999.

Carroll, Colleen. *The New Faithful: Why Young Adults are Embracing Christian Orthodoxy.* Chicago: LoyolaPress, 2002.

Carroll, Jackson W. *As One With Authority: Reflective Leadership in Ministry.* Louisville: Westminster John Knox Press, 1991.

Carroll, Jackson W., Barbara G. Wheeler, Daniel O. Aleshire, and Penny L. Marler. *Being There: Culture and Formation in Two Theological Schools.* New York: Oxford University Press, 1997.

Carroll, Jackson W., and Wade Clark Roof. *Bridging Divided Worlds: Generational Cultures in Congregations*. San Francisco: Jossey-Bass, 2002.

Census Bureau. 2004a. "Hispanic and Asian Americans Increasing Faster Than Overall Population." News release, U.S. Bureau of the Census. June 14, 2004.

Census Bureau. 2004b. "Census Bureau Projects Tripling of Hispanic and Asian Populations in 50 Years: Non-Hispanic Whites May Drop To Half of Total Population." News release, U.S. Bureau of the Census, March 18, 2004.

Chaves, Mark. *Congregations in America*. Cambridge, Mass.: Harvard University Press. 2004.

Chaves, Mark, Helen M. Giesel, and William Tsitsos. "Religious Variations in Public Presence: Evidence from the National Congregations Study." In *The Quiet Hand of God*. Edited by Robert Wuthnow and John H. Evans. Berkeley, Calif.: University of California Press, 2002.

Chaves, Mark, and Philip S. Gorski. "Religious Pluralism and Religious Participation." *Annual Review of Sociology* 27 (August 2001): 261–81.

Christiano, Kevin J., William H. Swatos Jr., and Peter Kivisto. *Sociology of Religion: Contemporary Developments*. Walnut Creek, Calif.: Altamira Press, 2002.

Clark, Terry Nichols, and Seymour Martin Lipset. *The Breakdown of Class Politics: A Debate on Post-Industrial Stratification*. Washington, D.C.: Woodrow Wilson Center Press; and Baltimore, Md.: The Johns Hopkins University Press, 2001.

Davie, Grace. *Europe: The Exceptional Case. Parameters of Faith in the Modern World*. London: Darton, Longman and Todd, 2002.

———. *Religion in Modern Europe: A Memory Mutates*. Oxford, England: Oxford University Press, 2000.

Davison, Kirsten Krahnstoever, Elizabeth J. Susman, and Leann Lipps Birch. "Percent Body Fat at Age 5 Predicts Earlier Pubertal Development Among Girls at Age 9." *Pediatrics* 111 (April 2003): 815–21.

Dear, Michael J., Editor, with J. Dallas Dishman. *From Chicago to LA: Making Sense of Urban Theory*. Thousand Oaks, Calif.: Sage Publications, 2002.

DeNavas-Walt, Carmen, and Robert W. Cleveland. *Money Income in the United States: 2001*. Current Population Reports, Consumer Income. U.S. Census Bureau. Washington, D.C.: Government Printing Office, September 2002.

DiMaggio, Paul, John Evans, and Bethany Bryson. "Have Americans' Attitudes Become More Polarized?" *American Journal of Sociology* 102 (November 1996): 690–755.

DiMaggio, Paul, and Walter Powell. "The Iron Cage Revisited: Institutional Isomorphism and Collective Rationality in Organizational Fields." *American Sociological Review* 48 (1983): 147–60.

———, eds. *The New Institutionalism in Organizational Analysis*. Chicago: University of Chicago Press, 1991.

Dudley, Carl S., and David A. Roozen. *Faith Communities Today: A Report on Religion in the United States*. Hartford, Conn: Hartford Institute for Religion Research, March 2001.

Ebaugh, Helen Rose, and Janet Saltzman Chafetz. *Religion and the New Immigrants: Continuities and Adaptions in Immigrant Congregations*. Walnut Creek, Calif.: AltaMira Press, 2000.

Eck, Diana L. *A New Religious America*. San Francisco: HarperSanFrancisco, 2001.

Eiesland, Nancy L. *A Particular Place: Urban Restructuring and Religious Ecology in a Southern Exurb*. New Brunswick, N.J.: Rutgers University Press, 2000.

Emerson, Michael O. "Beyond Ethnic Composition: Are Multiracial Congregations Unique?" Paper presented at the Society for the Scientific Study of Religion, Houston, October 2000.

Emerson, Michael O., and Karen Chai Kim. "Multiracial Congregations: An Analysis of Their Development and a Typology." *Journal for the Scientific Study of Religion* 42 (June 2003): 217–27.

Esping-Andersen, Gøsta, ed. *Changing Classes: Stratification and Mobility in Postindustrial Societies*. London: Sage Publications, 1993.

———. *Social Foundations of Postindustrial Economies*. Oxford, England: Oxford University Press, 1999.

Evans, John H. "Have Americans' Attitudes Become More Polarized? An Update." *Social Science Quarterly* 84 (March 2003): 71–90.

Finke, Roger, and Rodney Stark. *The Churching of America 1776–1990: Winners and Losers in Our Religious Economy*. New Brunswick, N.J.: Rutgers University Press, 1992.

Fischer, Claude S. "The Subcultural Theory of Urbanism: A Twentieth-Year Assessment." *American Journal of Sociology* 101 (November 1995): 543–77.

———. *To Dwell Among Friends: Personal Networks in Town and City*. Chicago: University of Chicago Press, 1982.

———. "Toward a Subcultural Theory of Urbanism." *American Journal of Sociology* 80 (May 1975): 1319–41.

Fischer, Claude S., and Michael Hout. *Different Places, Different People: The Redrawing of America's Social Geography.* "A Century of Difference" Working Paper, Berkeley, Calif.: University of California, 2003.

Flory, Richard W., and Donald E. Miller, eds. *GenX Religion.* New York: Routledge, 2000.

Furstenberg, Frank F., Jr., Sheela Kennedy, Vonnie C. McLoyd, Rubén G. Rumbaut, and Richard A. Settersten, Jr. "Growing Up Is Harder to Do." *Contexts* 1 (Summer 2004): 33–41.

Gallup, George, Jr. *Religion in America: Approaching the Year 2000.* Princeton, N.J.: Princeton Religion Research Center, 1990.

———. *The Unchurched American . . . 10 Years Later.* Princeton, N.J.: Princeton Religion Research Center, 1988.

Giddens, Anthony. *The Consequences of Modernity.* Stanford, Calif.: Stanford University Press, 1990.

Hadaway, C. Kirk. "Do Church Growth Consultations Really Work?" In *Church and Denominational Growth: What Does (and Does Not) Cause Growth or Decline.* Edited by David A. Roozen and C. Kirk Hadaway. Nashville: Abingdon Press, 1993.

Hadaway, C. Kirk, and Penny Long Marler. "All in the Family: Religious Mobility in America." *Review of Religious Research* 35 (December 1993): 97–116.

Hammond, Phillip E. *Religion and Personal Autonomy: The Third Disestablishment in America.* Columbia, S.C.: University of South Carolina Press, 1992.

Harris, Richard, and Robert Lewis. "Constructing a Fault(y) Zone: Misrepresentations of American Cities and Suburbs, 1900-1950." *Annals of the Association of American Geographers* 88, no. 4 (1998): 622–39.

Hauerwas, Stanley, and William H. Willimon. *Resident Aliens: Life in the Christian Colony.* Nashville: Abingdon Press, 1989.

Healy, Anthony E. "The Demise of Secularization." *Visions* 2, no. 3 (May–June 1999).

———. 2003a. "Sticking with It." *Visions* 6, no. 1 (January–February).

———. 2003b. "Full Adulthood Deferred." *Visions* 6, no. 2 (March–April).

Herberg, Will. *Protestant Catholic Jew: An Essay in American Religious Sociology.* Chicago: University of Chicago Press, 1983.

Hervieu-Léger. Danièlle. *Religion as a Chain of Memory.* Translated by Simon Lee. New Brunswick, N.J.: Rutgers University Press, 2000.

Hetzel, Lisa, and Annetta Smith. *The 65 Years and Over Population: 2000.*

Census 2000 Brief. U.S. Census Bureau. Washington, D.C.: Government Printing Office, October 2001.

Himes, Christine L. *Elderly Americans*. Louisville: Population Reference Bureau. December 2001.

Hobbs, Frank, and Nicole Stoops. *Demographic Trends in the 20th Century*. Census 2000 Special Reports, U.S. Census Bureau. Washington, D.C.: Government Printing Office, November 2002.

Hoge, Dean R., Benton Johnson, and Donald A. Luidens. *Vanishing Boundaries: The Religion of Mainline Protestant Baby Boomers*. Louisville: Westminster John Knox Press, 1994.

Hoge, Dean R., William D. Dinges, Mary Johnson, and Juan L. Gonzales. *Young Adult Catholics: Religion in the Culture of Choice*. Notre Dame, Ind.: University of Notre Dame Press, 2001.

Hopewell, James F. "Ghostly and Monstrous Churches." *Christian Century* (June 2, 1982).

Hout, Micheal, Andrew Greeley, and Melissa J. Wilde. "The Demographic Imperative in Religious Change in the United States." *American Sociological Review* 107 (September 2001): 468–500.

Hunter, James Davison. *American Evangelicalism: Conservative Religion and the Quandary of Modernity*. New Brunswick, N.J.: Rutgers University Press. 1983.

———. *Culture Wars: The Struggle to Define America*. New York: BasicBooks, 1991.

Iannaccone, Laurence R. "A Formal Model of Church and Sect." *American Journal of Sociology* 94 (1988): S241–68.

Jargowsky, Paul A. *Stunning Progress, Hidden Problems: The Dramatic Decline of Concentrated Poverty in the 1990s*. LivingCities Census Series. Washington, D.C.: Brookings Institution, May 2003.

Jasso, Guillermina, Douglas S. Massey, Mark R. Rosenzweig, and James P. Smith. "Exploring the Religious Preference of Recent Immigrants to the United States: Evidence from the New Immigrant Survey Pilot." Paper presented at the American Sociological Association annual meeting, Chicago, August 2002.

Jeung, Russell. "Asian American Pan-Ethnic Formation and Congregational Culture." In *Religions in Asian America: Building Faith Communities*. Edited by Pyong Gap Min and Jung Ha Kim. Walnut Creek, Calif.: AltaMira Press, 2002.

Kelley, Dean. *Why Conservative Churches Are Growing: A Study in Sociology of Religion*. New York: Harper & Row, 1972.

Lambert, Yves. "Religion in Modernity as a New Axial Age: Secularization or New Religious Forms?" *Sociology of Religion* (Fall 1999): 303–33.

Lamont, Michèle. *The Dignity of Working Men: Morality and the Boundaries of Race, Class, and Immigration.* New York: Russell Sage Foundation; and Cambridge, Mass.: Harvard University Press, 2000.

Laudarji, Isaac B., and Lowell W. Livezey. "The Churches and the Poor in a 'Ghetto Underclass' Neighborhood." In *Public Religion and Urban Transformation: Faith in the City.* Edited by Lowell W. Livezey. New York: New York University Press, 2000.

Lippman, Walter. "The Rock of Ages." In *Drift and Mastery.* Madison, Wis.: University of Wisconsin Press, 1990 (1914).

Livezey, Lowell W. "The New Context of Urban Religion." In *Public Religion and Urban Transformation: Faith in the City.* Edited by Lowell W. Livezey. New York: New York University Press, 2000.

Luhmann, Niklas. *Social Systems.* Translated by Dirk Baecker and John Bednarz Jr.. Stanford, Calif.: Stanford University Press, 1999.

Marler, Penny L., and C. Kirk Hadaway. "'Being Religious' or 'Being Spiritual' in America: A Zero-Sum Proposition?" *Journal for the Scientific Study of Religion* 41 (June 2002): 298–300.

Marty, Martin E. *Modern American Religion.* Vol. 2, *The Noise of Conflict, 1919–1941.* Chicago: University of Chicago Press, 1991.

———. "Public and Private: Congregation as Meeting Place." In *American Congregations.* Vol. 2, *New Perspectives in the Study of Congregations.* Edited by James P. Wind and James W. Lewis. Chicago: University of Chicago Press, 1998.

McConkey, Dale. "Whither Hunter's Culture War? Shifts in Evangelical Morality, 1988–1998." *Sociology of Religion* 62 (Summer 2001): 149–74.

McMillan, Becky R., and Matthew J. Price. *How Much Should We Pay the Pastor? A Fresh Look at Clergy Salaries in the 21st Century.* Pulpit and Pew Research Reports, no. 2. Durham, N.C.: Duke Divinity School, Winter 2003.

McPherson, Miller, Lyn Smith-Lovin, and James M. Cook. "Birds of a Feather: Homophily in Social Networks." *Annual Review of Sociology* 27 (2001): 415–44.

McRoberts, Omar M. *Streets of Glory: Church and Community in a Black Urban Neighborhood.* Chicago: University of Chicago Press, 2003.

Miller, Donald. *Reinventing American Protestantism: Christianity in the New Millennium.* Berkeley, Calif.: University of California Press, 1997.

Niebuhr, H. Richard. *The Purpose of the Church and Its Ministry.* New York: Harper & Row Publishers, 1956.

————. *The Social Sources of Denominationalism*. Gloucester, Mass.: Peter Smith, 1987.

Norton, Arthur J., and Louisa F. Miller. *Marriage, Remarriage and Divorce in the 1990s*. Current Population Reports, Special Studies. U.S. Census Bureau. Washington, D.C.: Government Printing Office, October 1992.

Noyelle, Thierry J., and Thomas M. Stanback Jr. *The Economic Transformation of American Cities*. Lanham, Md.: Rowan & Littlefield Publishers, Inc., 1984.

Numrich, Paul D. "Change, Stress, and Congregations in an Edge-City Technoburb." In *Public Religion: Faith in the City and Urban Transformation*. Edited by Lowell W. Livezey. New York: New York University Press, 2000.

Porterfield, Amanda. *The Transformation of American Religion: The Story of a Late Twentieth-Century Awakening*. New York: Oxford University Press, 2001.

Portes, Alejandro, and Rubén G. Rumbaut. *Immigrant America: A Portrait*, 2nd ed. Berkeley, Calif.: University of California Press, 1996.

————. *Legacies: The Story of the Immigrant Second Generation*. Berkeley, Calif.: University of California Press, 2001.

Price, Matthew. "After the Revolution: A Review of Mainline Protestant Clergy Leadership Literature Since the 1960s." *Theology Today* 59 (2002): 428–50.

Putnam, Robert D. *Bowling Alone: The Collapse and Revival of American Community*. New York: Simon & Schuster, 2000.

Richey, Russell E. "Denominations and Denominationalism: An American Morphology." In *Reimagining Denominationalism: Interpretive Essays*. Edited by Robert Bruce Mullin and Russell E. Richey. New York: Oxford University Press, 1994.

Roof, Wade Clark. *A Generation of Seekers: The Spiritual Journeys of the Baby Boom Generation*. San Francisco: HarperSanFrancisco, 1993.

————. *Spiritual Marketplace: Baby Boomers and the Remaking of American Religion*. Princeton, N.J.: Princeton University Press, 1999.

Roof, Wade Clark, and Mary Johnson. "Baby Boomers and the Return to the Churches." In *Churches and Denominational Growth*. Edited by David A. Roozen and C. Kirk Hadaway. Nashville: Abingdon Press, 1993.

Roof, Wade Clark, and William McKinney. *American Mainline Religion: Its Changing Shape and Future*. Rutgers, N.J.: Rutgers University Press, 1989.

Roozen, David A. "Denominations Grow as Individuals Join Congregations." In *Church and Denominational Growth: What Does (and Does Not) Cause Growth or Decline.* Edited by David A. Roozen and C. Kirk Hadaway. Nashville: Abingdon Press, 1993.

———. "Empty Nest; Empty Pew: The Boomers Continue through the Family Cycle." Revised paper. Hartford Institute for Religion Research, http://hirr.hartsem.edu/bookshelf/roozen_article1.html (accessed 1996).

Sargeant, Kimon Howland. *Seeker Churches: Promoting Traditional Religion in a Nontraditional Way.* New Brunswick, N.J.: Rutgers University Press, 2000.

Sassen, Saskia. "Desconstructing Labor Demand in Today's Advanced Economies." In *Laboring Below the Line.* Edited by Frank Munger. New York: Russell Sage Foundation, 2002.

———. *The Global City: New York, London and Tokyo,* 2nd ed. Princeton, N.J.: Princeton University Press, 2001.

Schachter, Jason. 2001a. *Geographic Mobility: Population Characteristics.* Current Population Reports. U.S. Census Bureau, Washington, D.C.: Government Printing Office, May 2001.

———. 2001b. *Why People Move: Exploring the March 2000 Current Population Survey.* Current Population Reports, Special Studies. U.S. Census Bureau. Washington, D.C.: Government Printing Office, May 2001.

Schaller, Lyle E. *Discontinuity and Hope: Radical Change and the Path to the Future.* Nashville: Abingdon Press, 1999.

Schmidley, Dianne. *The Foreign-Born Population in the United States: March 2002.* Current Population Reports, U.S. Census Bureau. Washington, D.C.: Government Printing Office, February 2003.

Sennett, Richard. *The Corrosion of Character: The Personal Consequences of Work in the New Capitalism.* New York: W.W. Norton & Company, 1998.

Shaw, Stephen J. "An Oak among Churches: St. Boniface Parish, Chicago, 1864–1990." In *American Congregations.* Vol. 1, *Portraits of Twelve Religious Communities.* Edited by James P. Wind and James W. Lewis. Chicago: University of Chicago Press, 1998.

Sherkat, Darren E. "Tracking the Restructuring of American Religion: Religious Affiliation and Patterns of Religious Mobility, 1973–1998." *Social Forces* 79 (June 2001): 1459–93.

Smith, Christian. *American Evangelicalism: Embattled and Thriving.* Chicago: University of Chicago Press, 1998.

Smith, Christian, Robert Faris, Melinda Lundquist Denton, and Mark Regnerus. "Mapping American Adolescent Subjective Religiosity and Attitudes of Alienation Toward Religion: A Research Report." *Sociology of Religion* 64 (March 2003) 111–13.

Smith, Denise. *The Older Population in the United States: March 2002*. Current Population Reports, U.S. Census Bureau. Washington, D.C.: Government Printing Office, April 2003.

Smith, R. Drew. "Churches and the Urban Poor: Interaction and Social Distance." *Sociology of Religion* 62 (Fall 2001): 301–13.

Smith, Vicki. "New Forms of Work Organization." *Annual Review of Sociology* 23 (1997): 315–39.

Sorkin, Michael, ed. *Variations of a Theme Park: The New American City and the End of Public Space*. New York: Hill and Wang, 2000.

Stark, Rodney. *The Rise of Christianity*. San Francisco: HarperCollins Publishers, 1997.

Stout, Harry S., and Catherine Brekus. "A New England Congregation: Center Church, New Haven, 1638–1989." In *American Congregations*. Vol. 1, *Portraits of Twelve Religious Communities*. Edited by James P. Wind and James W. Lewis. Chicago: University of Chicago Press, 1998.

Stump, Roger W. "The Effects of Geographical Variability on Protestant Church Membership Trends, 1980–1990." *Journal for the Scientific Study of Religion* 37 (December 1998): 636–51.

Tamney, Joseph B. *The Resilience of Conservative Religion: The Case of Popular, Conservative Protestant Congregations*. New York: Cambridge University Press, 2002.

Tamney, Joseph B., and Stephen D. Johnson. "The Popularity of Strict Churches." *Review of Religious Research* 39 (March 1998): 209–23.

Tamney, Joseph B., Stephen D. Johnson, Kevin McElmurry, and George Saunders. "Strictness and Congregational Growth in Middletown." *Journal for the Scientific Study of Religion* 42 (September 2003): 363–75.

Tracy, Gregory L. "Archdiocese to Lose 60 Churches." *The Pilot*. Newspaper of the Archdiocese of Boston, May 28, 2004.

Treas, Judith. *Older Americans in the 1990s and Beyond*. Population Bulletin, vol. 50. Washington, D.C.: Population Reference Bureau, March 1995.

Vaupel, James W., and Jim Oeppen. "Broken Limits to Life Expectancy." *Science* 296 (May 2002): 1029–31.

Wang, Youfa. "Is Obesity Associated With Early Sexual Maturation? A Comparison of the Association in American Boys Versus Girls."

Pediatrics 110 (November 2002): 903–10.

Warner, R. Stephen. "Changes in the Civic Role of Religion." In *Diversity and Its Discontents: Cultural Conflict and Common Ground in Contemporary American Society*. Edited by Neil J. Smeiser and Jeffrey C. Alexander. Princeton, N.J.: Princeton University Press, 1999.

———. "Coming to America: Immigrants and the Faith They Bring." *Christian Century* (February 10, 2004).

———. 1998a. "Immigration and Religious Communities in the United States." In *Gatherings in Diaspora: Religious Communities and the New Immigration*. Edited by R. Stephen Warner and Judith G. Wittner. Philadelphia: Temple University Press, 1998.

———. 1998b. *New Wine in Old Wineskins: Evangelicals and Liberals in a Small-Town Church*. Berkeley, Calif.: University of California Press, 1990.

———. 1998b. "The Place of the Congregation in the Contemporary American Religious Configuration." In *American Congregations*. Vol. 2, *Perspectives in the Study of Congregations*. Edited by James P. Wind and James W. Lewis. Chicago: University of Chicago Press, 1998.

———. "Work in Progress Toward a New Paradigm for the Sociological Study of Religion in the United States." *American Journal of Sociology* 98 (March 1993): 1044–93.

Warner, R. Stephen, and Judith G. Wittner, eds. *Gatherings in Diaspora: Religious Communities and the New Immigration*. Philadelphia: Temple University Press, 1998.

Weber, Max. *The Protestant Ethnic and the Spirit of Capitalism*. Translated by Talcott Parsons. London: Routledge Classics, 2002 (1930).

———. *The Sociology of Religion*. Translated by Ephraim Fischoff. Boston: Beacon Press, 1993.

Wedam, Elfriede. "Catholic Spirituality in a New Urban Church." In *Public Religion and Urban Transformation: Faith in the City*. Edited by Lowell W. Livezey. New York: New York University Press, 2000.

———. "The 'Religious District' of Elite Congregations: Reproducing Spatial Centrality and Redefining Mission." *Sociology of Religion: A Quarterly Review* 64, no. 1 (Spring 2003): 47–64.

Weeks, Louis B. "The Incorporation of the Presbyterians." In *The Organizational Revolution: Presbyterians and American Denominationalism*. Edited by Milton J. Coalter, John M. Mulder, and Louis B. Weeks. Louisville: Westminster John Knox Press, 1992.

Wheeler, Barbara G. *Is There a Problem? Theological Students and Religious Leadership for the Future*. Auburn Studies. New York: Auburn Theological Seminary, 2001.

Wilson, William Julius. *The Truly Disadvantaged: The Inner City, the Underclass, and Public Policy*. Chicago: University of Chicago Press, 1987.

Winter, Gibson. *The Suburban Captivity of the Churches*. New York: Doubleday, 1961.

Woodhead, Linda. *How Liberal Is Liberal Christianity? Why Humanization Is Not the Same as Subjectivization*. Paper presented at the annual meeting of the Association for the Sociology of Religion, Atlanta, August 2003.

Woolever, Cynthia. "U.S. Congregational Life Survey: What Did We Learn About Worshipers?" Paper presented at the annual meeting of the Society for the Scientific Study of Religion, Salt Lake City, October 2002.

Woolever, Cynthia, and Deborah Bruce. *A Field Guide to U.S. Congregations: Who's Going Where and Why*. Louisville: Westminster John Knox Press, 2002.

Wuthnow, Robert. *After Heaven: Spirituality in America Since the 1950s*. Berkeley, Calif.: University of California Press. 1998.

———. *Christianity in the 21st Century: Reflections on the Challenges Ahead*. New York: Oxford University Press, 1993.

———. "Religious Involvement and Status-Bridging Social Capital." *Journal for the Scientific Study of Religion* 41 (December 2002): 669–84

———. *The Restructuring of American Religion: Society and Faith Since World War II*. Princeton. N.J.: Princeton University Press, 1989.

Yang, Fenggang. *Chinese Christians in the United States: Conversion, Assimilation, and Adhesive Identities*. University Park, Pa.: The Pennsylvania State University Press, 1999.

———. "Chinese Conversion to Evangelical Christianity: The Importance of Social and Cultural Contexts." *Sociology of Religion* 59 (Fall 1998): 237–57.

Yu, Eui-Young. "The Growth of Korean Buddhism in the United States with Special Reference to Southern California." In *Korean Americans and Their Religions: Pilgrims and Missionaries from a Different Shore*. Edited by Ho-Youn Kwon, Kwang Chung Kim, and R. Stephen Warner. University Park, Pa.: The Pennsylvania State University Press, 2001.